GCSE
Questions and Answers

BIOLOGY

KEY STAGE 4

Jackie Callaghan & Morton Jenkins

Chief Examiners

SERIES EDITOR: BOB McDUELL

Letts

EDUCATIONAL

Contents

HOW TO USE THIS BOOK

The aim of the *Questions and Answers* series is to provide you with help to do as well as possible in your exams at GCSE or, in Scotland, at General and Credit levels. This book is based on the idea that an experienced Examiner can give, through examination questions, sample answers and advice, the help students need to secure success and improve their grades.

This *Questions and Answers* series is designed to provide:

● Introductory advice on the different types of question and how to answer them to maximise your marks.

● Information about the other skills, apart from the recall of knowledge, that will be tested on examination papers. These are sometimes called **Assessment Objectives** and include communication, problem solving, evaluation and interpretation (see pages 5–6). The *Questions and Answers* series is intended to develop these skills by showing you how marks are allocated.

● **Revision Summaries** to remind you of the topics you will need to have revised in order to answer examination questions.

● Many examples of **examination questions**, arranged by topic, with spaces for you to fill in your answers, just as on an examination paper. Only try the questions once you have revised a topic thoroughly. Read the Revision Summary before attempting the questions to double-check you know the topic. It is best not to consult the answers before trying the questions.

● **Sample answers** to all of the questions.

● **Advice from Examiners**. By using the experience of actual Chief Examiners we are able to give advice on how you can improve your answers and avoid the most common mistakes.

THE IMPORTANCE OF USING QUESTIONS FOR REVISION

Past examination questions play an important part in revising for examinations. However, it is important not to start practising questions too early. Nothing can be more disheartening than trying to do a question which you do not understand because you have not mastered the topic. Therefore, it is important to have studied a topic thoroughly before attempting any questions on it.

How can past examination questions provide a way of preparing for the examination? It is unlikely that any question you try will appear in exactly the same form on the papers you are going to take. However, the Examiner is restricted on what can be set because the questions must cover the whole syllabus and test certain Assessment Objectives. The number of totally original questions that can be set on any part of the syllabus is very limited and so similar ideas occur over and over again. It certainly will help you if the question you are trying to answer in an examination is familiar and you know you have done similar questions before. This is a great boost for your confidence and confidence is what is required for examination success.

Practising examination questions will also highlight gaps in your knowledge and understanding which you can go back and revise more thoroughly. It will also indicate which sorts of questions you can do well.

Attempting past questions will get you used to the type of language used in questions.

Finally, having access to answers, as you do in this book, will enable you to see clearly what is required by the examiner, how best to answer each question, and the amount of detail required. Attention to detail is a key aspect of achieving success at GCSE.

EXAMINATION TECHNIQUE

Success in GCSE examinations comes from proper preparation and a positive attitude to the examination. This book is intended to help you overcome 'examination nerves' which often come from a fear of not being properly prepared. Examination technique is extremely important and certainly affects your performance. Remember the basics:

● Read the questions carefully.

● Make sure that you watch the time carefully and complete the paper. It is no good answering one question well if you spend so long doing it that you do not answer another question at all.

● Read the rubric on the front of the examination paper carefully to make sure you know how many questions to attempt.

● Examination papers usually tell you how many marks are available for each answer. Take notice of this information as the number of marks gives a guide to the importance of the question and often to the amount which you ought to write.

● Check before the end of the examination that you have not missed any pages. Remember to turn over the last page, too.

● Remember to leave time to check through your work carefully.

DIFFERENT TYPES OF EXAMINATION QUESTION

Structured questions

These are the most common questions used at GCSE level in biology. The questions are divided into parts (a), (b), (c), etc, and the parts are often subdivided into (i), (ii), etc. There is a structure built into each question which can usually be recognized as beginning with the easiest parts and becoming progressively demanding towards the end.

For each part of the question there are a number of lines or a space for your answer. This is a guide to the amount of detail required for the answer. If you should need more space, continue your answer on a separate piece of paper which will be supplied on request. Remember to label any extra paper with the correct question number.

For each part of the question, the number of marks available is shown in brackets e.g. (3). If a part is worth three marks, the answer needs to be more than one or two words. You would usually be expected to write three points to gain three marks.

To give you a guide as you work through structured questions, the papers are usually designed to enable you to score one mark per minute. A question worth 5 marks should therefore take about five minutes to answer.

Questions are designed to assess more skills than just recall, including:

(a) using **symbolic representations** – testing the skill of the student to understand and use graphical information and models of biological information;

(b) using **observation** – testing the ability to decide the relevant features of a problem and using observed patterns to make predictions;

(c) **interpretation and application** – where actual data is presented to the student to test the skill of producing hypotheses consistent with the data, and assessing the validity of such hypotheses.

Keep your answers as concise as possible. An examiner may not be able to see that you have the right idea of the answer if it is written in an overcomplicated way.

Free-response questions

These can include essay questions. In this type of question, you are able to develop your answer in different ways. You can write as much as you wish. Candidates often do not write enough, or they 'pad out' their answer with irrelevant information. Remember, you can only score marks when your answer matches the marking points on the Examiner's mark scheme.

In free-response questions it is important to plan your answer before starting it, allocating the correct amount of time to each part of the question. Attention to spelling, punctuation and grammar is important, especially the correct use and spelling of technical terms. This is something you should check at the end of the examination if you have time to spare.

Sample question

> Name one form of atmospheric pollution. State its source and explain its effects on the environment. (6)
>
> Suggest ways of reducing this form of pollution. (2)

This question should take about eight to ten minutes to answer. You need to choose a form of atmospheric pollution of which you have detailed knowledge.

Plan

Nitrogen oxides and acid rain would be a good choice.

- State the form of pollution and its source.
- Explain how these chemicals react in the atmosphere to form acid rain.
- Explain the effects of acid rain on living organisms and buildings.
- State ways of reducing this pollution.

Here is a sample answer.

Oxides of nitrogen, NO and NO_2 (NO_x), enter the air from the exhausts of motor vehicles. *(1 mark for the name of the pollutant and 1 mark for its source)*

Nitrogen dioxide reacts with water vapour and oxygen in the air to form nitric acid. This becomes part of a cloud and eventually falls as acid rain or acid snow. *(1 mark for a description of how acid rain is formed)*

The acid rain reacts with minerals in the soil, making them soluble. These minerals are then leached from the topsoil and plants cannot obtain these nutrients. *(1 mark for the effect of acid rain on plants)*

The acidic water and certain metal ions which leach from the soil enter rivers and lakes. Fish suffer because the effects of excess acidity prevent their eggs hatching and also interfere with gaseous exchange at the gills. *(1 mark for the effect of acid rain on fish)*

Acid rain causes corrosion to stonework by dissolving limestone. *(1 mark for the effect of acid rain on buildings)*

Lime (calcium hydroxide) can be added to lakes to neutralize some of the acid. Pollution by nitrogen oxides is reduced when catalytic converters are fitted to vehicle exhausts. These cause the exhaust fumes to break down into nitrogen, water and carbon dioxide. Nitrogen is present in the atmosphere and is not a pollutant. *(2 marks for suggesting ways to reduce pollution)*

TERMS USED IN QUESTIONS

Sometimes candidates find difficulty in understanding the meaning of instructions given in questions. The following table contains a list of common terms which often introduce questions on examination papers, together with an explanation of each.

Instruction in question	Meaning
Describe	Extended prose, merely stating observations
Give an account of	Write an explanatory description
Discuss	Give an account of the various views on a topic
Compare	Put side by side, one or more similarities
Contrast	Put side by side, one or more differences
Distinguish between	A combination of 'compare' and 'contrast'
Explain/Account for	Extended prose, giving reasons for observations
State	A brief statement with no supporting evidence
Define	State precisely and concisely what is meant
Suggest	Give examples or explanations where there may be more than one correct answer. You could apply your answer to a situation outside the syllabus
Summarize	Give a brief account of
Survey/Outline	Give a general (as opposed to detailed) account of
Comment on	Make explanatory remarks or criticisms on
Illustrate by reference to	Use named examples to demonstrate the idea or principle

ASSESSMENT OBJECTIVES IN BIOLOGY

Assessment Objectives are the intellectual and practical skills you should be able to show. Opportunities must be made by the Examiner when setting the examination paper for you to demonstrate your mastery of these skills when you answer the question paper.

Traditionally the Assessment Objective of knowledge and understanding has been regarded as the most important skill to develop. Candidates have been directed to learn large bodies of knowledge to recall in the examination. Whilst not wanting in any way to devalue the learning of facts, it should be remembered that on modern papers knowledge and understanding can only contribute about half of the marks available. The other half of the marks are acquired by mastery of the other Assessment Objectives, namely:

- Communicate scientific observations, ideas and arguments effectively.
- Select and use reference materials and translate data from one form to another.
- Interpret, evaluate and make informed judgements from relevant facts, observations and phenomena.
- Solve qualitative and quantitative problems.

1 Communicate scientific observations, ideas and arguments effectively
(weighting on papers approximately 5–10%)

In any examination, communication of information to the Examiner is of primary importance. This Assessment Objective should not be confused with spelling, punctuation and grammar (SPAG) – up to 5% added to your mark in coursework for the quality of your spelling, punctuation and grammar.

Questions are built into the paper to test your ability to communicate scientific information. Often these questions require extended answers.

In this type of question it is important to look at your answer objectively after you have written it and try to judge whether your answer is communicating information effectively.

2 Select and use reference materials and translate data from one form to another *(weighting on papers approximately 10–15%)*

In questions testing this Assessment Objective you are asked frequently to pick information from a chart or table and use it in another form, e.g. to draw a graph, a pie chart, bar chart, etc. You may be asked to complete a table using information from a graph.

It is important to transfer the skills you have acquired in Mathematics to your work in Biology.

Skill acquired	Approx. grade in GCSE Maths
Read information from graphs or simple diagrams	F
Work out simple percentages	F
Construct and use pie charts	F
Use graphs	E
Plot graphs from data provided. The axes and scales are given to you.	E
Be able to draw the best line through points on a graph	C
Select the most appropriate axes and scales for graph plotting	B

It is reasonable, therefore, to conclude that at Higher level you might be required to use a blank piece of graph paper and choose your own scales and axes. Then you would plot the points and draw a line of best fit through the points. If you are doing this, remember:

❶ To draw your graph as large as possible on the graph paper by choosing scales appropriately. Avoid choosing scales where, for example, 3 small squares are equivalent to 5°C. It would be better if 1 small square was equivalent to 1°C or 2°C. With this type of graph drawing, marks are usually awarded for the choice of scales and for labelled axes.

❷ To plot each point with a dot or small cross. Circle the dot or cross to make its position clear.

❸ Your line of best fit, whether it is a straight line or a curve, does not have to go through all the points. Some points may not be in the correct place, even if you plotted them correctly, because of inaccuracies in the experiment or experimental error.

On a Foundation tier paper a similar graph may have to be drawn but it would be more appropriate for the Examiner to provide a grid with axes and scales given. Then you would only have to plot the points and draw the line of best fit. It would probably be worth fewer marks than a graph on the Higher tier paper.

3 Interpret, evaluate and make informed judgements from relevant facts, observations and phenomena (*weighting on papers approximately 10–15%*)

Questions testing this Assessment Objective are often difficult for candidates. It is much easier to test this on a Higher tier paper than on a Foundation tier paper.

The command word 'suggest' is very frequently used as the information given, perhaps in a paragraph, table, diagram or any combination of these, is open to more than one interpretation.

Look carefully at all of the information given and look for possible alternative interpretations before writing your answer.

4 Solve qualitative and quantitative problems (*weighting on papers approximately 10–15%*)

Again opportunities to test this Assessment Objective are greater, especially for solving quantitative problems, on Higher tier papers.

Qualitative problems can include describing the effects of humans on the environment or applications of Biology. Quantitative problems include genetics and ecological energy transfer. Remember, when attempting to carry out a calculation, to:

❶ Use all of the information given to you. If the question gives energy values, they should be used.

❷ Show all of your working so credit can be given if you do not get the correct answer but get some way through the question.

❸ Give correct units to your answers if there are units.

You will see questions throughout this book where the question is designed to test Assessment Objectives other than knowledge and understanding.

Energy and life

Plants and some bacteria are the only organisms that can make food. Animals either eat plants or they eat other animals which themselves have eaten plants.

The process by which plants make food is called **photosynthesis.** Plants use inorganic materials, in particular *carbon dioxide* from the atmosphere and *water* from the soil, and in the presence of *chlorophyll* and *energy* (in the form of sunlight) they manufacture *carbohydrates*.

Photosynthesis can be divided into two basic stages:

❶ *Splitting water* using energy from the sun.

❷ *Reduction of carbon dioxide* by the addition of hydrogen.

Stage 1

Energy from sunlight, trapped by the green pigment *chlorophyll*, splits water molecules into oxygen and hydrogen, the process of **photolysis**.

$$4H_2O \xrightarrow[\text{Chlorophyll}]{\text{Sunlight}} 4[OH] + 4[H]$$

$$4[OH] \longrightarrow 2H_2O + O_2 \text{ (by-products)}$$

Stage 2

The hydrogen is combined with carbon dioxide in a complex series of reduction reactions. The product acts as a starting point for the manufacture of most carbohydrates, proteins, fats and most vitamins. The significance of photosynthesis to animals is thus:

● It provides the source of their dietary requirements.

● It provides them with oxygen (given off in Stage 1).

● It uses the carbon dioxide that they produce as waste during respiration.

Respiration is the release of *energy* from *glucose* and occurs in all living cells.

$$\underset{\substack{\text{Glucose} \quad \text{Oxygen}}}{C_6H_{12}O_6 + 6O_2} \xrightarrow{\text{Enzymes}} \underset{\substack{\text{Carbon dioxide} \quad \text{Water} \quad \text{ATP}}}{6CO_2 \quad + \quad 6H_2O \quad + \quad \text{Energy}}$$

The equation is a gross over-simplification of the process because:

❶ Many other intermediate enzyme-controlled reactions occur.

❷ Most of the oxidation takes place by the action of hydrogen carriers removing hydrogen from the glucose, then oxygen is added during the final stage only.

❸ Energy is liberated in a succession of stages, a small amount at a time.

❹ The energy is in *adenosine triphosphate* (ATP), which acts as an energy carrier. ATP carries energy to the cell, then releases the energy. During this release of energy, ATP loses one of its phosphate groups to become *adenosine diphosphate* (ADP).

Respiration and gaseous exchange

Respiration is the chemical process which releases *energy* from *glucose* in every living cell during oxidation.

In mammals, gaseous exchange takes place between the lungs and the blood. This is made possible by breathing. In simple animals, individual cells are in direct contact with the environment. The more complex forms have blood to transport materials.

Atmospheric pressure and concentration of gases in the air both play important roles in the diffusion of gases through membranes. Another vital property of gases is the ability to dissolve in water. Oxygen, in the alveoli of the lungs, diffuses into the blood stream.

Metabolism involves respiration and the growth process. The rate at which it occurs during rest is called the basal metabolic rate.

REVISION SUMMARY

Since oxygen is needed for the complete oxidation of glucose, this type of respiration is called **aerobic respiration**. Sometimes respiration takes place without the use of oxygen. This process is called **anaerobic respiration**. Yeast respires anaerobically by converting glucose into ethanol.

Glucose → Ethanol + Carbon dioxide + Energy

This is called alcoholic fermentation.

During strenuous exercise, we are unable to breathe fast enough for oxygen to be supplied to our muscles. Our muscles obtain energy from anaerobic respiration. In this process, *lactic acid* is formed.

Glucose → Lactic acid + Energy

Lactic acid is a mild poison and causes muscles to ache. When the exercise is finished, oxygen is needed to break down the lactic acid into carbon dioxide and water. The oxygen needed to break down lactic acid is called the **oxygen debt**. Alcoholic fermentation and anaerobic respiration produce less energy than aerobic respiration.

Excretion

Various wastes result from protein metabolism. They are removed from the body through *kidneys*, *skin*, and *lungs*. The kidneys are the body's most important excretory organs. They filter practically all the nitrogenous wastes from blood. The skin also excretes wastes. It gets rid of water, salts, and some urea in sweat. In addition, sweat helps control your body temperature.

Response and movement

The **central nervous system** is composed of the *brain* and the *spinal cord*. They communicate with all parts of the body via nerves.

There are three types of nerve cell or neurone.

❶ *Sensory neurones* which carry messages from the *receptors* (sense organs) to the spinal cord and brain (the central nervous system).

❷ *Effector neurones* (motor neurones) carry messages from the central nervous system (CNS) to the *effectors* (muscles or glands).

❸ *Connector neurones* (relay neurones) carry messages through the CNS between the sensory neurones and effector neurones.

Sense organ	Stimulus it is sensitive to
Skin	touch, pressure, pain, heat, cold
Eye	light
Ear	vibrations
Nose	chemicals in solution
Tongue	chemicals in solution

Movement in humans is brought about by *antagonistic pairs* of muscles acting across joints and pulling on bones which act as levers.

The control of the muscles is by conscious effort, when it is *voluntary*, and involves the central nervous system. However, there are also rapid, *reflex*, protective actions which involve movement but do *not* require conscious effort. The following table gives some examples of reflex actions.

Reflex	Stimulus	Response
Coughing	Irritant in the throat	Contraction of abdominal muscles and expiratory intercostal muscles; relaxation of the diaphragm
Swallowing	Food at the back of the throat	Soft palate is raised; epiglottis is closed; peristalsis takes place
Blinking	Object coming towards the eye	Contraction of eyelid muscles
Knee-jerk	Pressure/pain on knee	Contraction of flexor muscles
Pupil contraction/dilation	Change in light intensity	Contraction of muscles of the iris

Drugs and the nervous system

Tobacco is not addictive in the sense that narcotic drugs are. However, it does pose serious health problems, as it tends to shorten life and seems to contribute to many diseases.

Alcohol is a depressant. Used excessively, it leads to alcoholism. Alcohol can cause organic diseases which may be fatal. It can be antisocial and is dangerous when used by people who drive.

Misuse of **drugs** can be harmful to the users and may even cause death. Drug addiction can be a psychological problem, a physical one, or both. *Narcotic drugs* can become physically addictive. People who take them habitually often do so in order to escape from problems. This is psychological addiction. But as the body builds up a drug tolerance, so addicts must take more and more in order to 'escape'. Physically, the body demands more in order to avoid painful *withdrawal symptoms*. Narcotics are illegal, with just a few available on prescription. Consequently, many addicts spend much of their time looking for ways to obtain drugs and invariably turn to crime, which creates problems for both them and society in general.

Chemical control

Ductless glands are called **endocrine glands**. They secrete *hormones* directly into the blood stream.

Glands are controlled by their influence on each other, by feedback, and by the nervous system. Their delicate balance is maintained by *homeostatic mechanisms*. If any one of the endocrine glands slows down or becomes overactive, the chemical balance is upset and the body reacts, making the person feel ill.

Nutrition

Our bodies need a variety of complex organic nutrients. They also need minerals, water and fibre. There are three kinds of organic nutrients that are needed in bulk: carbohydrates, fats and proteins.

The digestive system is a tube divided into various regions. This tube is called the alimentary canal. Each region is a specialized organ. Each organ is adapted for performing certain phases of the digestive process. Both our teeth and muscles in the alimentary canal break down the food we eat, mechanically. Many glands pour enzymes into the digestive tract. These enzymes break food down chemically. These mechanical and chemical changes must take place before food can be absorbed and used by our body cells.

If you need to revise this subject more thoroughly, see the relevant topics in the *Letts* GCSE Biology Study Guide or CD-ROM.

1 (a) The diagram below shows part of the human digestive system.

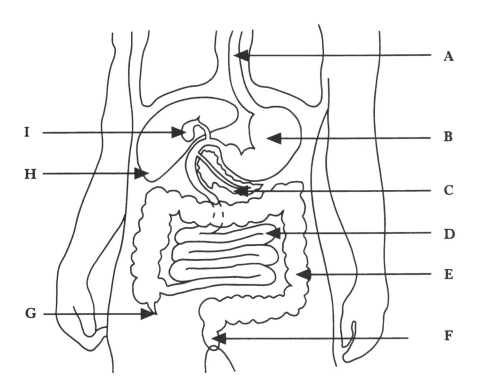

(i) Complete the table by inserting letters from the diagram to identify the named parts of the digestive system.

Part of digestive system	Letter
Liver	
Pancreas	
Oesophagus	
Appendix	

(4)

(ii) Describe **one** function of the part labelled **E**.

.... (1)

(iii)Describe two features of the small intestine which help in the absorption of the products of digestion.

1. ....

2. .... (2)

(b) The table below gives the percentages of different types of tissue found in the body of a typical male adult.

Body tissues	Mass (%)
Muscle	45
Bone	15
Fat (essential)	3
Fat (storage)	12
Other tissues	25

Part of this information is presented in Pie Chart 1 below.
Pie Chart 2 shows the percentage for a typical female adult.

Pie Chart 1
Typical Male Adult

Pie Chart 2
Typical Female Adult

(i) Complete Pie Chart 1, using the information from the table. (2)

(ii) Which tissue has the greatest percentage mass in both males and females?

.... (1)

(iii) Which adult contains more fat in total?

.... (1)

(iv) A man weighs 80 kilograms. Calculate the expected mass of the muscle tissue in his body.

.... kg (1)

SQA 1995

2 (a) A group of pupils carried out an experiment to illustrate digestion in mammals.
1. The pupils mixed 20cm³ of starch suspension with 5cm³ of 'digestive juice' in a beaker.
2. They immediately tested a sample of the mixture for the presence of starch and for maltose.
3. They took a second sample after 15 minutes and again carried out the tests for starch and maltose.

Time	Starch	Maltose
At start	present	absent
After 15 minutes	absent	present

(i) Name the enzyme present in the digestive juice.

.... (1)

(ii) Name a part of the digestive system in a mammal where this enzyme is produced.

.... (1)

(b) The list below contains statements about enzyme activity.

List
1. Substrate of an enzyme
2. Optimum conditions for an enzyme
3. Enzyme action is specific
4. Increased rate of chemical reaction
5. Products of enzyme action

(i) Using pH as your example, explain the meaning of **statement 2**.

....

.... (1)

(ii) Select all the statements from the list above which relate to **each** of the following sentences.

A statement can be used **once**, **more than once** or **not at all**.

	Statement Numbers
The enzyme pepsin acts only on protein molecules.	
Protein molecules are broken down to form short chains of amino acids.	

(2)

SQA 1995

3 The diagram below represents part of the structure of the hip joint.

(a) Complete each of the boxes with the name or function of the part of the joint indicated.

Name	Function
	Holds the bones of a joint together

Name	Function
Cartilage	

Name	Function
Synovial fluid	

Femur

(2)

(b) Explain why two muscles are needed to control the movements of the bones of a hinge joint.

....

....

....

.... (2)

SQA 1995

4 The diagram shows a section through the leaf of a green plant.

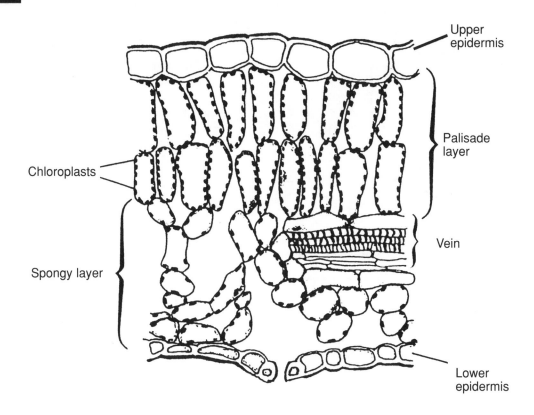

(a) (i) Which layer of this leaf contains most chloroplasts?

    .... (1)

    (ii) Which layer of this leaf will receive most sunlight?

    .... (1)

(b) How do the air spaces in the leaf help it to photosynthesise well?

    ....

    ....

    .... (3)

SEG 1995

5 Insulin-secreting cells can be injected into a person's abdomen. The cells are in jelly capsules and a single treatment could replace daily injections of insulin for several months. The jelly capsule allows insulin molecules to pass through but keeps out antibodies and white blood cells.

(a) Where, in the body, is insulin normally produced?

.... (1)

(b) Name the condition which is treated by the method described above.

.... (1)

(c) State why this condition cannot be **cured** by injecting insulin.

.... (1)

(d) What would be the effect of (i) antibodies and (ii) white blood cells if they were able to pass through the jelly to the cells?

(i)   Antibodies   (1)

(ii)   White blood cells   (1)

(e) Explain why glucagon has the opposite effect to insulin.

....

....

....

.... (3)

(f) The production of insulin by biotechnology involves the following steps. They are in the wrong order. Use the letters A-E to show below the correct order.

A   Separating and purifying insulin.
B   Putting the gene into the genetic material of bacteria.
C   Identifying the human gene controlling the production of insulin.
D   Isolating the gene which controls the production of insulin.
E   Growing large numbers of genetically altered bacteria.

.... (5)

(g) State one advantage of using insulin made by biotechnology.

.... (1)

WJEC 1996

6 (a) The diagram below shows a single kidney tubule.

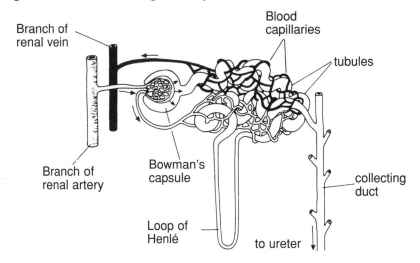

(i) In which region of a kidney are the Bowman's capsules situated?

.... (1)

(ii) Explain why the liquid trickling down the Loop of Henlé does **not** contain glucose even though the Bowman's capsule does.

.... (1)

(iii) Name the liquid in the collecting duct.

.... (1)

(b) Desert rats can live on diets without water for long periods but normal rats cannot. The graph below shows the concentration of urea in urine produced by both types of rats when given the same diets.

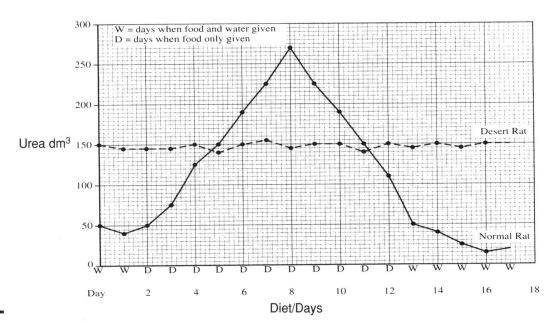

(i) State the concentration of urea produced in the urine of the normal rat at 8 days.

.... (1)

(ii) Calculate the difference in the concentration of the urea produced by both rats when they have had no water for eight days.

....

.... (1)

(iii) What change is seen in the working of the kidneys of normal rats after nine days?

.... (1)

(iv) Urea contains nitrogen. Name the class of food which should be reduced in the diet for a smaller amount of urea to be produced.

.... (1)

The diagram below shows a simplified version of a kidney dialysis machine.

dialysis solution

dialysis tubing

(c) Name the process by which substances pass from the dialysis tubing into the solution.

.... (1)

(d) What do you notice about the direction of the flow of blood and the dialysis solution? Explain the advantage of this arrangement.

....

.... (1)

(e) Explain why red blood cells remain inside the dialysis tubing.

.... (1)

Cell growth and reproduction

Organisms grow by **mitosis**.

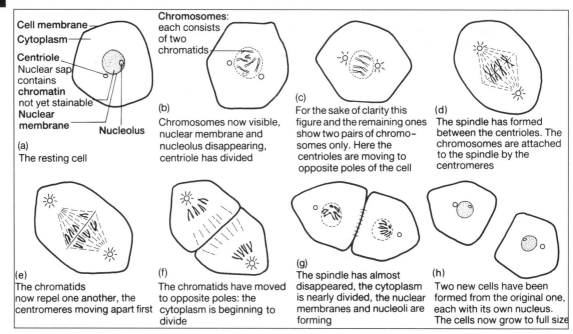

Stages in mitosis

Each daughter cell produced in mitosis has the *diploid chromosome number*. Further, the chromosomes of the daughter cells are identical to those of the mother cell. All body cells in all members of the same species contain the same kind and number of chromosomes.

Sperms and eggs are produced by a different kind of division, known as **meiosis**.

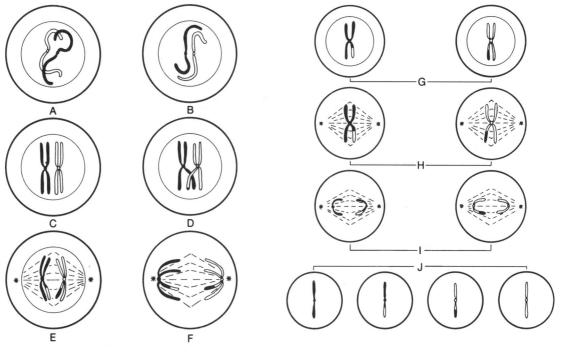

Key: Maternal chromosome is white
Paternal chromosome is black; Diploid number = 2

Meiosis in a gamete-forming cell

The stages in meiosis, as shown in the previous diagram, are as follows:

❶ Each *chromosome* moves towards, and begins to pair with, its partner. The pairing process results in a very *close contact* along the whole of the length of the chromosomes (B). Thus the first stage of *meiosis* differs from that in mitosis. At the start of mitosis the chromosomes consist of two chromatids which are formed by duplication, but in meiosis whole *pairs* of chromosomes come together.

❷ While in this close union, the chromosomes shorten and thicken, and each becomes *duplicated* into **two chromatids** (C). At this stage the *nuclear membrane* begins to disintegrate.

❸ Along the length of the pairs of chromosomes, individual **chromatids cross** one another in complex ways. As a result of this, chromatids **exchange** various sections (D). The force of attraction that up to this point has held the pairs of chromosomes together now ceases to operate fully, and the pairs of chromosomes begin to *separate* (E). (In the diagram for simplicity only one cross-over is shown.)

❹ The chromosomes separate completely and move to *opposite* poles of the cell (F). The *cytoplasm divides* (G). At this point, each daughter cell still has the *diploid* number of chromosomes, but because of *crossing over* of sections of the chromatids, **genes** from one partner have been mixed with genes from the other partner.

❺ Each new cell undergoes a *mitotic* division. The chromosomes, each consisting of *two complete chromatids* (even though parts have been exchanged), line up along the centre of the new cell (H). One set of chromatids passes to each pole of the cell. Each new set of chromosomes starts to form a nucleus (I).

❻ A division of the cytoplasm occurs and nuclear membranes reappear. As a result, **four gametes**, each with the *haploid* number of chromosomes, have been formed from an original *diploid* cell (J).

The *significance* of meiosis is:

(a) The formation of cells with **half** the diploid number of chromosomes.

(b) **Mixing of genes** between pairs of chromosomes contributing to **variation** within the chromosomes.

Meiosis involves two stages of division. The cells that result contain the *haploid chromosome number*. When these cells join in fertilization, the diploid number is restored.

Principles of heredity

It was the work of Gregor Mendel (1822–1884) with garden peas that opened up the field of **heredity** to science. Mendel's hypotheses about **genes**, which he called factors, have become basic principles of **genetics**. Among these principles are the ideas that genes:

● control heredity,

● occur in pairs, and

● may be *dominant* or *recessive*.

The genetic material

Many years have passed since Gregor Mendel's experiments with garden peas opened up the science of genetics. Since 1900, scientists have probed deeper and deeper into the mysteries of the living cell and its genetic material. Most of the traits we inherit are necessary and helpful. Some are harmful. We are finding out more and more about these genetic problems. Often, learning the cause of a problem leads to its correction. We are beginning to learn the effects of genes in causing such disorders as cystic fibrosis, Huntington's chorea, haemophilia and many other conditions.

Genes sometimes *mutate* and a major cause of mutations is high energy radiation. Radiation from artifical sources and natural sources will cause changes in the structure of genes, leading to mutation.

In the body cells of mammals, one of the pairs of chromosomes carries the genes which determine gender. These are called sex chromosomes. In females, the sex chromosomes are the same (XX); in males the sex chromosomes are different (XY). The X chromosome can carry more genes than the Y chromosome and some of these genes do not have a corresponding partner on the Y chromosome in males. Such genes are said to be sex-linked. If these genes are harmful in their recessive form, they can cause males to suffer certain disorders, allowing females to carry the gene where it is masked by its dominant form. If the female has the dominant 'normal' gene, then she will not suffer from the disorder.

Many disorders are inherited in humans by being caused by genes having been passed from parents to children.

Cystic fibrosis (abnormal bronchiole and pancreas function) can be passed on by parents, neither of whom has the disease, because it is caused by a recessive gene. Each parent could have the dominant gene masking the recessive.

N = normal (dominant); n = cystic fibrosis (recessive)

Parents	Nn		x	Nn	
Children	NN	Nn		Nn	nn

The child with the nn genotype would suffer from cystic fibrosis, i.e. a 25% chance.

Huntington's chorea (muscle spasms and speech impairment) is passed on by one parent who has the disease because it is caused by a dominant gene.

H = Huntington's chorea (dominant); h = normal (recessive)

Parents	Hh		x	hh	
Children	Hh	Hh		hh	hh

The children with the Hh genotype would suffer from Huntington's chorea, i.e. a 50% chance.

Haemophilia (inability of the blood to clot) is passed on to sons by females who do not suffer from the disorder.

XX = female; XY = male

H = normal blood clotting (dominant); h = haemophilia (recessive)

Parents	$X^H X^h$		x	$X^H Y$	
Children	$X^H X^H$	$X^H Y$		$X^h X^H$	$X^h Y$

The children with the $X^h Y$ genotype would suffer from haemophilia, i.e. 25% chance or a 50% chance in sons.

Applied genetics

If you need to revise this subject more thoroughly, see the relevant topics in the *Letts* **GCSE Biology Study Guide or CD-ROM.**

For many centuries, people have worked at breeding improved strains of plants and animals. Three important methods of breeding are **mass selection**, **hybridization**, and **inbreeding**. Mass selection involves choosing the parents for further breeding from a large number of individuals. Hybridization is the crossing of two different strains. An example of inbreeding is self pollination in plants. Over several generations, the offspring with the desired traits are sorted out by mass selection. In the end, a pure strain is produced.

Another form of applied genetics is **genetic engineering**. This relies on isolating a useful gene from one organism and putting it into another of a different species. For example, scientists often isolate genes from human chromosomes which control the production of certain hormones. They put these useful genes into bacteria or yeast cells. The human genes are transferred to the bacteria or yeast to increase production of the hormone. The microbes multiply very rapidly and can be cultured relatively cheaply. In fact, they can provide almost unlimited amounts of substances that are practically unobtainable in bulk in any other way.

1 The information below is about insulin.

• Insulin is a *hormone*, produced by the pancreas, which reduces the concentration of glucose in the blood.

• People who cannot produce insulin, or not enough of it, are called diabetics.

• Diabetics usually need daily injections of insulin.

• For many years this insulin has been extracted from the pancreas of pigs, sheep and cattle.

• Scientists can now produce human insulin using a technique known as genetic-engineering.

(a) What are *hormones*?

....

....

....(2)

(b) The diagram below shows some of the stages involved in the production of genetically-engineered human insulin.

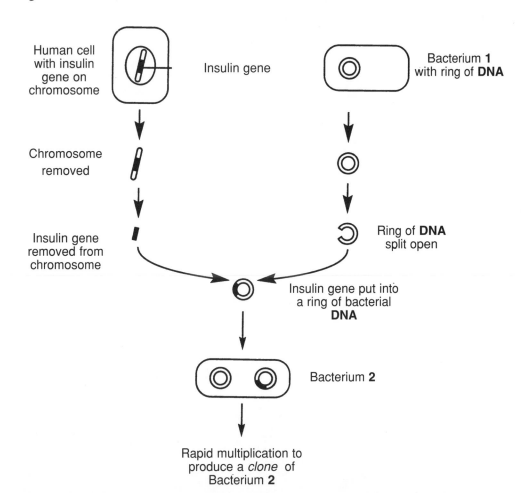

QUESTIONS

(i) How is the insulin gene removed from the human chromosome?

.... (1)

(ii) The *clone* of bacterium **2** produces large quantities of insulin.

   (A) What is a *clone*?

   ....

   .... (2)

   (B) Explain why bacteria are suitable organisms to use for this purpose.

   ....

   ....

   ....

   .... (3)

(c) Explain **one** advantage genetically-engineered insulin has compared with that extracted from animals.

   ....

   .... (2)

SEG 1995

2 (a) In the fruit fly wing type is controlled by one pair of alleles. The diagram shows two types of wings, normal and vestigial.

Fruit flies

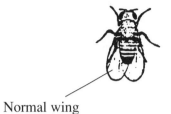

Normal wing

Vestigial wing

The normal winged fly is heterozygous and the vestigial winged fly is homozygous.

Explain the meaning of:

homozygous

....

.... (1)

heterozygous

....

.... (1)

(b) A normal winged fly of unknown genotype was crossed with a vestigial winged fly. The allele for normal wing, **A**, is dominant to the allele for vestigial wing, **a**. The offspring are shown below.

(i) From the diagram determine the ratio of normal winged flies to vestigial winged flies.

.... (1)

(ii) Give the genotype of this normal winged parent fly.

.... (1)

NICCEA 1995

3 The diagram below shows the inheritance of eye colour in a family. The gene for brown eyes is dominant (**B**) and the gene for blue eyes is recessive (**b**).

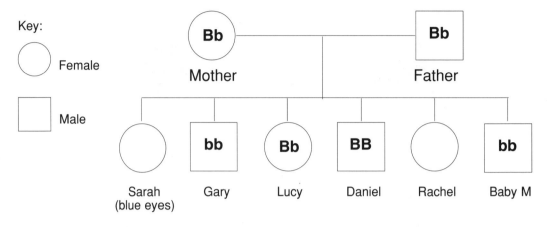

Key:

◯ Female

▢ Male

Mother **Bb** ——— Father **Bb**

| Sarah (blue eyes) | Gary **bb** | Lucy **Bb** | Daniel **BB** | Rachel | Baby M **bb** |

(a) Which of the following statements is true?

    A Lucy and Daniel both have blue eyes

    B Lucy and Daniel have different coloured eyes

    C Lucy and Daniel have the same coloured eyes

    D All the males in the family have brown eyes

    Answer: statement...................is true   (1)

(b) What is the sex and eye colour of baby M?

    .... (2)

(c) (i) Daniel's **genotype** is **BB**. What is Sarah's **genotype**?

    .... (1)

    (ii) Explain how you worked out your answer.

    .... (1)

In this family, Rachel has an identical twin. Rachel has brown eyes.

(d) (i) Who is Rachel's identical twin?

    .... (1)

    (ii) Explain how you decided on your answer.

    .... (2)

LONDON 1995

4 Busy Lizies are small plants which are easily grown and produce large numbers of white, pink or red flowers all through the summer.

(a) In Busy Lizies the allele for red flowers (**R**) is dominant to the allele for white flowers (**r**).

A red-flowered Busy Lizie (**RR**) was cross-pollinated with a white-flowered Busy Lizie (**rr**). The seeds produced by this cross were grown to produce an **F1** generation of plants all with red flowers.

(i) What is meant by cross-pollination?

....

....

.... (2)

(ii) Why did all the **F1** generation of plants have red flowers?

....

....

.... (2)

(iii) Two of these **F1** red-flowered plants were cross-pollinated. The resulting seeds were grown to produce an **F2** generation of plants.

Use a genetic diagram to explain the genotypes and phenotypes of the **F2** plants.

You will be awarded up to **two** marks for the clarity of your genetic diagram.

....

....

....

....

....

.... (6)

(b) Imagine that on a remote, uninhabited island scientists discovered colonies of Busy Lizies growing and that most of these plants produced blue flowers.

These plants could have evolved as a result of *natural selection* in action on a *mutant* **blue**-flowering Busy Lizie plant.

(i) Explain how a *mutant* (genetic mutation) can arise by referring to the way DNA replicates.

....

....

....

.... (3)

(ii) Explain how *natural selection* could have produced these colonies of **blue**-flowering Busy Lizie plants

....

....

....

....

....

....

....

.... (3)

SEG 1995

Many people used to take **natural resources** for granted. We have wasted many of these resources and caused thousands of hectares of land to become useless.

REVISION SUMMARY

- An increase in population has caused mass property development and a need to increase crop yields.

- The increased use of fertilizers, pesticides, silage, etc. has had an adverse effect on the environment, often because the chemicals involved in these treatments find their way into water.

- Over-use of land has caused *soil erosion*.

- An increase of industry and transport has increased *air pollution*: e.g. emissions of sulphur dioxide and oxides of nitrogen cause acid rain; carbon dioxide increases the *Greenhouse Effect* and CFCs damage the ozone layer.

  Large numbers of people, as well as industry, cause pollution problems. Pollution can be defined as anything which, when added to the environment, destroys its purity.

- **Biodegradable substances** are broken down by *bacteria*. This releases minerals for *recycling*. However, there is a limit as to how much can be taken care of in this way.

- Non-biodegradable substances are not broken down. In fact, they may be toxic to organisms in the environment.

- Air can be polluted by many chemicals, some of which are poisonous to plants and animals.

- Radioactive particles can cause tissue damage and death. It is most important that people realize the effects of human action and do something about them.

The population of the world as a whole has been *growing steadily*, though in individual countries there have been *fluctuations* in population size as people have migrated to newly discovered territories or have gone off in search of new food and mineral sources. Malthus, in 1798, suggested that because the population *increases faster* than food production there should be some sort of **birth control**. The growth of the world's population is now much faster than it has been in the past for the following reasons:

❶ The **increased effectiveness of medical science in saving lives** and virtually wiping out many formerly fatal diseases, such as *diphtheria* and *smallpox*.

❷ Practically all mothers and babies survive childbirth because of **improved pre- and post-natal medical care**.

❸ Increased lifespan in the Western industrial countries due to a **better diet** than that enjoyed by our ancestors.

❹ **Agricultural development**.

❺ **Industrial development** due to technological advances leading to greater potential for trade and greater affluence.

Two consequences of an increasing population growth rate are:

- **shortage of food**,

- **pollution**.

If you need to revise this subject more thoroughly, see the relevant topics in the *Letts* GCSE *Biology Study Guide* or *CD-ROM*.

1 The diagram shows the percentage of males and females, at different ages, in a population in 1840.

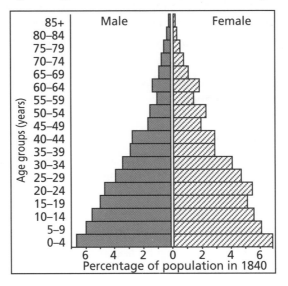

(a) (i) Which age group has the largest percentage in the male population?

.... (1)

(ii) What percentage of the male population is between 25 and 29 years of age?

.... (1)

(iii) Give **three** reasons why many people did **not** live longer than 35 years of age.

1. ....

2. ....

3. .... (3)

The diagram shows the percentage of males and females in the same population in 1970.

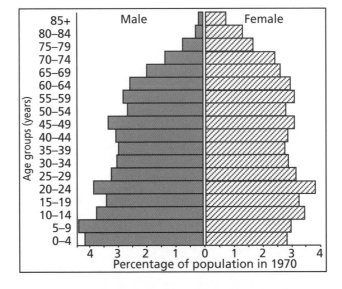

(b) (i) Give **one** difference between the male and female population for people over 55 years of age in 1970.

.... (1)

(ii) Explain why the population graphs for 1840 and 1970 are different shapes.

.... (1)

(iii) Give **two** problems associated with overpopulation.

1. ....

2. .... (2)

NICCEA 1995

2 Carbon Dioxide (CO_2) gas is found in the atmosphere.

(a) (i) Name a process which removes CO_2 from the atmosphere.

.... (1)

The burning of fossil fuels releases CO_2 into the atmosphere.

(ii) State one other way in which CO_2 is released into the atmosphere.

.... (1)

Other petroleum 3%
Fuel oil 9%
Gas oil 4%
Diesel 6%
Natural Gas 19%
Petrol 13%
Other emissions 4%
Coal 42%

Figure 1 Carbon dioxide emissions by type of fuel, 1990 UK

(iii) Study Figure 1. What was the source of the **largest proportion** of the carbon dioxide emitted by machinery using fuel in 1990?

.... (1)

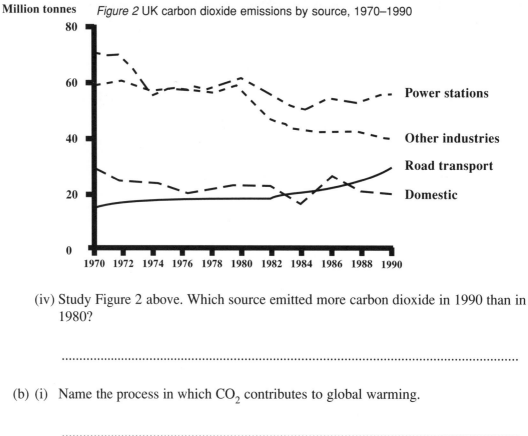

Million tonnes   *Figure 2* UK carbon dioxide emissions by source, 1970–1990

(iv) Study Figure 2 above. Which source emitted more carbon dioxide in 1990 than in 1980?

.... (1)

(b) (i) Name the process in which CO_2 contributes to global warming.

.... (1)

(ii) Explain how this process leads to a rise in global warming.

....

....

....

....

....

....

....

.... (4)

NEAB 1996

3 (a) The table shows some information about what have become known as the 'greenhouse gases'.

Name	Source	Influence on Greenhouse Effect (%)
Carbon dioxide	burning forests burning fossil fuels cement production	56
CFCs (chlorofluorocarbons)	refrigerators air conditioning systems aerosol propellant	23
Methane	rotting vegetation waste gases from animals, e.g. cows, sheep	14
Nitrous oxide	breakdown of organic and inorganic fertilizers	7

(i) On the graph below plot the data showing the influence of each gas on the greenhouse effect. The percentage for carbon dioxide has already been plotted for you.

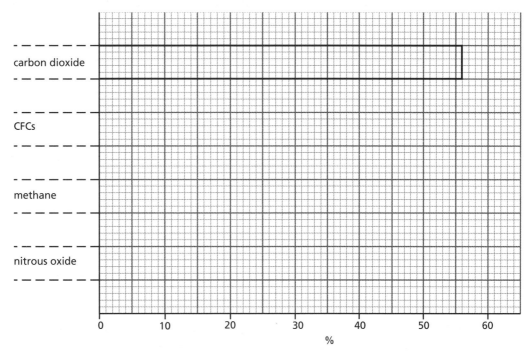

(3)

(ii) On the evidence in the table, which of the greenhouse gases are products of natural processes?

.... (2)

(iii) In light of the data in the table, suggest why the following should be encouraged:
    1 the development of renewable energy devices such as windmills;
    2 better insulation of houses;
    3 planting more trees.

....

....

....

....

....

.... (6)

(b) In 1800 there were 280 parts per million of carbon dioxide in the atmosphere. In 1990 there were 350 parts per million and this is expected to rise to 560 by the year 2030.

  (i) How much more carbon dioxide was in the air in 1990 compared to 1800?

.... (1)

  (ii) The predicted rise in carbon dioxide concentration in the period from 1990 to 2030 is 310 parts per million.
      Suggest an explanation for the difference between this value and your answer to (i).

....

....

.... (2)

MEG 1994

4 Five groups of students carried out an experiment to show how sulphur dioxide affected the growth of cress seedlings. Each group set up its experiment as shown in the diagram.

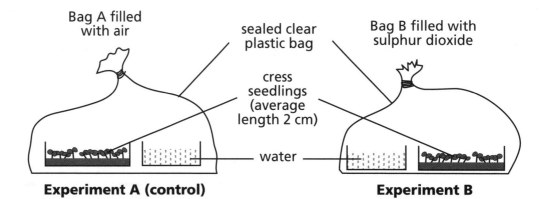

Bag A filled with air   sealed clear plastic bag   Bag B filled with sulphur dioxide

cress seedlings (average length 2 cm)

water

Experiment A (control)   **Experiment B**

(a) (i) Using the diagram, state how Experiment B is different from the control experiment.

....

.... (1)

(ii) State one reason why a control was set up.

....

....

....

.... (2)

(iii) Each group measured the length of all their seedlings, then calculated the average length. Explain why the average length of seedlings was recorded.

....

....

.... (2)

(b) After seven days the students recorded the average length of the seedlings. The results are shown in the diagram.

Group number	Average length of cress seedlings (cm)	
	Experiment A	Experiment B
1	8.2	3.0
2	10.0	4.2
3	6.4	6.4
4	7.6	3.5
5	5.8	2.8

Complete the graph for Experiment B by constructing bars. Use the shading shown in the key for Experiment B.
Experiment A (the control) has been plotted for you. (3)

Bar chart to show average length of cress seedlings

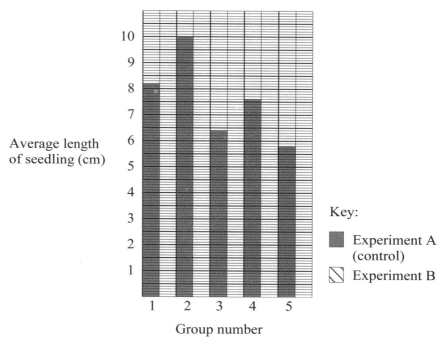

(c) (i) One group made a mistake in setting up the experiment.
State which group made a mistake and give a reason for your answer.

Group.............................

Reason...

.... (3)

(ii) Study the table of results shown in 4(b) and write a conclusion for this experiment.

....

....

....

....

.... (4)

(iii) Describe other environmental effects that occur when sulphur dioxide emissions are released into the atmosphere.

....

....

....

....

.... (4)

NEAB 1995

5   In 1992 elephants living on the shores of Lake Kariba in Zimbabwe were slowly starving because they lost the use of their muscular trunks to obtain food. They had a problem with floppy trunks. All the affected elephants lived in the area of Zimbabwe subjected to severe drought. The drought caused the lake to become smaller. Lake Kariba is used for fishing, tourism and water sports but not for human water supplies. Lead fishing weights, petrol, exhaust fumes, discarded batteries and oil filters from boats are all sources of lead pollution. Lead is a poisonous metal which affects the nervous system.

Use the information above and your knowledge of pollution to answer the following:

(a) State the link between drought and the effects of lead pollution on the elephants.

....

.... (1)

(b) Suggest why the elephants' trunks were floppy.

....

....

.... (2)

(c) Describe how lead pollution in the lake might affect humans.

....

....

....

.... (2)

(d) The graph shows changes in the size of a protected population of elephants in Zimbabwe, over a period of eleven years.

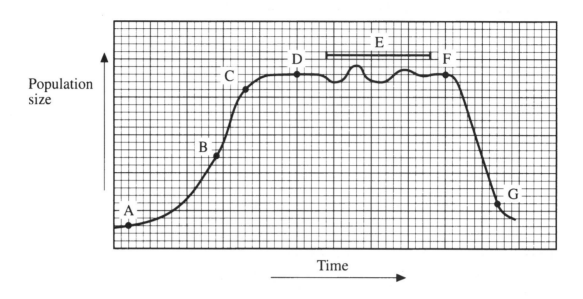

Complete the table by writing a letter from the graph which correctly identifies **each** factor affecting population size.

Factors affecting population size	Letter
Birth rate and death rate are equal	
Short-term environmental change (drought)	
Population growing without limits	
Effects of lead pollution being seen	

(4)

WJEC 1996

All organisms depend on their surroundings to stay alive.

There is a thin layer of life starting a few feet below the ground and extending through the lower atmosphere of our planet. It is called the *biosphere*. It may be considered as one huge *ecosystem*. Or, it may be divided into many small ecosystems. An *ecosystem* is an environment in which living and non-living things affect one another. It is also a system in which materials are recycled. Living organisms are the community. Groups of the same kind of organisms are called populations.

The non-living part of the ecosystem is called the *physical environment* or *habitat*. It has much influence on the biotic community.

A stable population density is important to a balanced ecosystem. Many factors can change population density. Lack of food, for example, will cause a population to decrease. Removal of natural enemies will usually make it temporarily increase. These same factors influence human population density.

Physical factors of an environment (abiotic factors)

❶ Light intensity is particularly important because of its function in photosynthesis.

❷ Oxygen and carbon dioxide are important because of their functions in respiration and photosynthesis, respectively.

❸ Temperature is important because of the influence it has on the rate of chemical reactions going on in all living things.

❹ A balanced supply of minerals is essential to all living things as part of their nutrition.

❺ Water is essential because it makes up a large proportion of protoplasm and all chemical reactions in living things take place in solution.

Biotic factors

All living organisms have some influence upon the outside environment of their neighbours. This influence may be small, such as in a limited competition for water or light. On the other hand it may be very great. For example, many animals play an important part in the outside environment of plants. Some animals pollinate flowers; others disperse seeds; some are the carriers of plant disease; some trample vegetation. Among animals, humans have had the greatest impact on the environment of other organisms.

The total outside environment, consisting of both abiotic and biotic factors, determines which species come together to form a natural community in any one place.

Life in communities

Three sorts of relationships are recognized:

❶ **Competition**: may be between the many members of a given species, or between members of different species.

❷ **Dependence**: all animals are dependent on plants for a supply of food and oxygen.

❸ **Interdependence**: while some organisms compete with one another, and some are totally dependent upon others, there are some ways in which all the species in a community are interdependent.

If you need to revise this subject more thoroughly, see the relevant topics in the *Letts* GCSE Biology Study Guide or CD-ROM.

1 The drawing shows a freshwater aquarium in a laboratory.

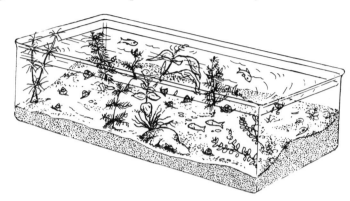

(a) The diagram shows a food web for some of the organisms which live in this aquarium.

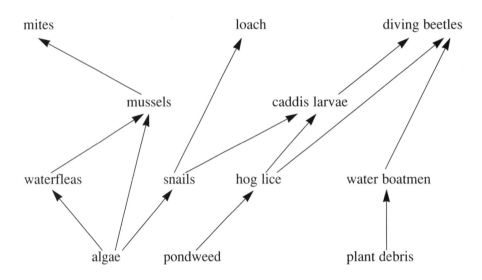

Use the information from the food web to construct a food chain which contains four organisms.

....

.... (2)

(b) (i) Give four factors which might affect the size of the population of algae in the aquarium.

1. ....

2. ....

3. ....

4. .... (4)

(ii) Explain how an increase in the population of algae might affect the population of

1. the water fleas:

....

....

2. the mussels:

....

.... (4)

(c) There are two loach in the aquarium. These are fish about 5 cm in length which feed on snails. There are 30 snails in the aquarium. These are 5 mm in diameter and they feed only on algae. Algae are single-celled plants about 1/100 mm in diameter.

Construct and label a pyramid of numbers for the above organisms.

(2)

(d) The organisms which live in the aquarium make up a community. They use the materials in the aquarium, but the amounts of materials do not change very much.

Explain as fully as you can how this balance is maintained.

....

....

....

....

.... (2)

NEAB 1995

2 (a) Name the energy source on which all living things on Earth depend.

.... (1)

(b) List **three** environmental factors which affect the speed at which microbes bring about decay.

1. ....

2. ....

3. .... (3)

Study the information below and answer questions (c) (i) to (iv).

The figure below shows the change in population of deer living on a plateau in Arizona.

Between 1906 and 1923 thousands of predators of the deer such as wolves were killed by wildlife managers.

(c) (i) What was the normal capacity of the plateau between 1905 and 1926?

....deer (1)

(ii) Suggest what the term normal capacity means here.

....

.... (1)

(iii) In which year was the deer population at the normal capacity for the plateau?

.... (1)

(iv) How did the size of the deer population change between 1907 and 1924? Suggest an explanation for this change.

....

....

....

.... (2)

MEG 1995

3. The table below shows some animals and examples of the food they eat.

Animal	lacewing fly	small bird	fox	weasel	vole	hawk
Food the animal eats	greenfly	lacewing fly, caterpillars	small birds, voles	voles	plants	small birds

(a) Complete the boxes A, B, C and D in the food web below with names of animals from the table.

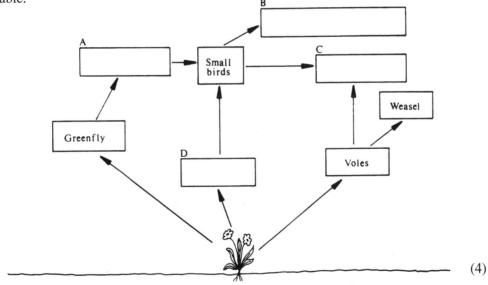

(b) Underline the word which describes the plant in the food web.

DECOMPOSER, PRODUCER, HERBIVORE, CARNIVORE (1)

(c) (i) Where does the energy for this food web come from?

.... (1)

(ii) Name the process which makes this energy available to plants.

.... (1)

(d) What might happen to the weasels and the plants if all the voles died?

Weasels:

.... (1)

Plants:

.... (1)

(e) A stoat is an animal which looks like a weasel and eats similar food.
Suggest and explain the change in the population of one named animal in the food web if stoats were released in the area.

Animal

....

Change

....

.... (3)

LONDON 1995

4 The diagram shows the energy flow through a food chain.

Wastes   Heat

```
                    ┌──────────────────────┐
                    │ 1kJ converted into   │
                    │ a tertiary consumer  │
                    └──────────────────────┘
59 kJ  ◄─── X ──────────────┬────── Y ──►  90 kJ
                    ┌──────────────────────┐
                    │ 150 kJ converted into│
                    │ a secondary consumer │
                    └──────────────────────┘
600 kJ ◄─── X ──────────────┬────── Y ──►  1750 kJ
                    ┌──────────────────────┐
                    │ 2500 kJ converted into│
                    │ a primary consumer   │
                    └──────────────────────┘
10 000 kJ ◄─── X ───────────┬────── Y ──►  37 500 kJ
                    ┌──────────────────────┐
                    │ 50 000 kJ converted into│
                    │       producer       │
                    └──────────────────────┘
```

Use the information in the diagram to help answer the following questions.

(a) What processes, in the consumers, account for the energy flow represented by the letters X and Y?

X ....

Y .... (2)

(b) What percentage of the energy available in the primary consumer is available for the secondary consumer? (Show your working.)

Percentage available .... (2)

(c) Why are there rarely more than five trophic levels in a food chain?

....

....

.... (2)

NICCEA 1995

REVISION SUMMARY

Most microbes are not harmful to mankind. Some are essential to maintain life as we know it, and others are exploited by us in biotechnology when they are used in the production of various foods, ethanol, antibiotics, and biogas.

Essential microbes

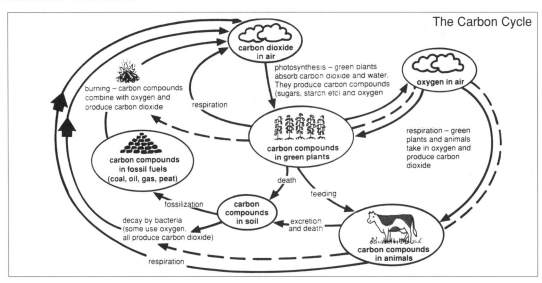

The Carbon Cycle

Carbon dioxide is taken from the environment by green plants during photosynthesis. The carbon is used to make carbohydrates, lipids (fats), and proteins. When these plants are eaten, the carbon enters the food chain. Some of the carbon becomes carbon dioxide during respiration and is returned to the environment.

When organisms die, microbes feed on them and carbon dioxide is released as carbon dioxide as the microbes respire. The recycling of carbon is called the **carbon cycle**.

In order to be able to make proteins, plants must also obtain nitrogen as nitrates by way of their roots. When microbes break down the waste products of animals and the protein in dead organisms, they make ammonium compounds.

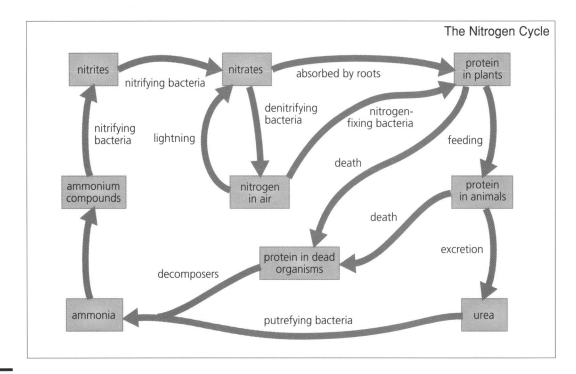

The Nitrogen Cycle

Nitrifying bacteria change ammonium compounds into nitrates. **Nitrogen-fixing bacteria** living in the roots of certain plants can change nitrogen from the air into nitrates. **Denitrifying bacteria** can replace nitrogen in the air by breaking down nitrates.

This constant recycling of nitrogen is called the nitrogen cycle. Without it, the world supply of protein would stop.

Microbes and biotechnology

Biotechnology uses microbes to make substances for us or to do work for us.

Certain types of bacteria are used in the production of some foods.

In the production of yoghurt, bacteria are added to milk at 30°C. The bacteria ferment the milk sugar, producing **lactic acid**. This causes the milk protein to become solid.

The single-celled fungus, yeast, can respire without oxygen, fermenting sugar to produce ethanol and carbon dioxide. In baking bread, a mixture of yeast and sugar is mixed with dough (flour and water). The mixture is left in a warm place to allow the yeast to respire rapidly. The carbon dioxide produced makes the bread rise. The bread is then baked in an oven.

In the production of the **antibiotic**, penicillin, a culture of the fungus, *Penicillium*, is added to a solution containing sugar in a large vessesl called a fermenter. During the first 24 hours, the fungus rapidly grows. When the sugar in the medium becomes less, the fungus begins to produce penicillin. After 7 days, the medium is filtered and the penicillin removed.

Biogas, mainly methane, is produced by **anaerobic fermentation** of organic matter by microbes. Biogas production can be on a large scale so that it can be used as a fuel.

Ethanol-based fuels can be produced by the anaerobic fermentation of extracts of sugar cane with the use of yeast. Ethanol is distilled from the products and the resulting liquid can be used as fuel in motor vehicles.

Harmful microbes

Disease-causing microbes are called **pathogens** and include: viruses, bacteria, fungi, and single-celled animals called protozoa. Depending on the type, they can be spread through the air, by direct contact, through food and water, and by carriers such as insects.

The body has natural defence mechanisms including natural **immunity**. Artificial immunity may be acquired through vaccination.

A **vaccine** contains **antigens** derived from a pathogen. They cause the blood to produce **antibodies** which protect against infection by any future invasion by the pathogen. There are five common ways of producing a vaccine:

- using the killed pathogen, e.g. whooping cough;
- using a live weakened (attenuated) strain of the pathogen, e.g. tuberculosis, rubella;
- chemically modifying a toxic (poison) molecule so that it is no longer poisonous but still resembles the shape of the toxic molecule, e.g. diphtheria and tetanus;
- separating antigens from the microbe and using them as a vaccine, e.g. influenza;
- using genetically engineered bacteria to mass produce antigens, e.g. hepatitis B.

If you need to revise this subject more thoroughly, see the relevant topics in the *Letts* GCSE Biology Study Guide or CD-ROM.

1 The diagram below shows part of the nitrogen cycle.

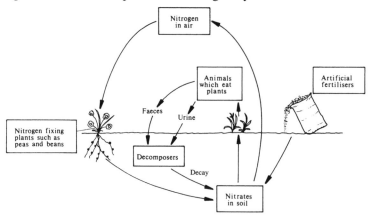

(a) (i) What is meant by the term **decay?**

....

....

.... (2)

(ii) Name a type of organism which causes decay.

.... (1)

(b) What is meant by the term **nitrification**?

....

....

.... (2)

(c) The process of denitrification is shown but not named on the diagram. What is the end product of denitrification?

.... (1)

(d) Organic farmers do not use artificial fertilisers to put nitrates into the soil.

(i) Explain why organic farmers often grow more peas and beans than other farmers.

....

....

.... (2)

(ii) Explain why **organic** farmers often keep farm animals even if they mainly grow crops such as wheat.

....

.... (1)

LONDON 1995

2 Some students investigated the production of alcohol from sugars by yeast. They used solutions of the same concentration of four different sugars, **P**, **Q**, **R**, and **S**. For each sugar they set up the apparatus as in diagram **A**. The length of the bubble of carbon dioxide shown in diagram **B** was measured every five minutes for each apparatus. The temperature was kept at 25°C. The amount of carbon dioxide indicates the amount of alcohol produced.

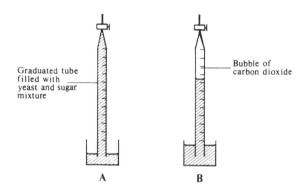

Graduated tube filled with yeast and sugar mixture

Bubble of carbon dioxide

A   B

The table below shows the results of the investigation.

Mixture	Length of CO_2 bubble at 5 minute intervals (cm)						
	5 mins	10 mins	5 mins	20 mins	25 mins	30 mins	30 mins
Yeast + Sugar P	3.0	10.0	17.0	26.0	35.0	38.0	40.0
Yeast + Sugar Q	0.5	1.0	1.5	2.0	2.0	2.0	2.0
Yeast + Sugar R	0.5	1.0	1.0	1.5	1.5	1.5	1.5
Yeast + Sugar S	4.0	11.0	19.0	27.0	36.0	40.0	42.0
Yeast + Water	0.5	0.5	0.5	1.0	1.0	1.0	1.0

(a) (i) Why was the yeast and water mixture included in the experiment?

.... (1)

(ii) Which sugar produced most alcohol?

.... (1)

QUESTIONS

(iii) Why was it important that the tubes were **completely** filled with the yeast and sugar mixture at the start of the experiment?

.... (1)

(iv) Why did the rate of production of carbon dioxide slow down after a time?

.... (1)

(b) Suggest **two** ways in which the rate of alcohol production could have been increased.

1. ....

2. .... (2)

(c) Yeast lives naturally on fruit. Some of the sugars (P, Q, R and S) came from animals. Suggest which of these sugars came from animals. Give a reason for your answer

....

....

.... (2)

LONDON 1995

3 The diagram shows a sewage treatment plant.

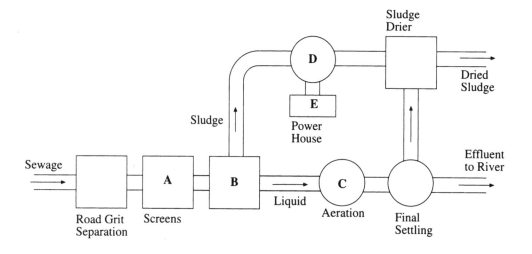

(a) (i) Suggest the function of the screens at **A**.

....

.... (1)

(ii) Outline what occurs at:

B ....

....

C ....

....

D ....

.... (3)

(b) (i) What passes from D to E ?

.... (1)

(ii) What may happen to the sludge when it is removed from the treatment plant?

....

.... (1)

(c) Some bacteria in a sewage treatment plant change ammonium compounds to nitrates.
What type are they ?

.... (1)

(d) **Explain** what would happen to the water in a lake if untreated sewage enters it.

....

....

....

.... (2)

WJEC 1996

Water relations in plants

Water is the most important factor in a flowering plant's environment. The amount of water in an environment is critical in determining what types of plants will survive there.

Plants need water for almost all of the processes that go on inside them.

In photosynthesis, water supplies the hydrogen that combines with carbon dioxide to form carbohydrates. Water also plays a key role in providing a solvent for materials in cytoplasm of cells.

Also, water is the medium of transport of materials in plants. Manufactured foods and minerals, from the soil, are dissolved in water to be carried up and down in the **xylem** and **phloem**. Finally, water in the vacuoles of cells make them firm as a result of turgor pressure. This helps support non-woody plants.

Water balance in plants

In order to survive, an organism must remain in a state of balance with its environment. An important factor for this balance is the movement of materials in and out of cells. All of these materials must pass through the cell membrane.

The cell membrane is **selectively permeable**, i.e. different molecules and ions pass through it in different amounts and at different rates. Foods, water, wastes and other materials selectively pass through the membrane. Cytoplasm and stored foods are retained within the membrane.

Diffusion controls the movement of many molecules through the membrane and may be described as the spreading out of molecules from a region of greater concentration to one of lesser concentration. Diffusion of water is called **osmosis** and is the spreading of water molecules through a selectively permeable membrane from a region of greater concentration of water molecules to one of lesser concentration. When concentrations are the same on both sides of the selectively permeable membrane, the rate of movement of water molecules is equal in both directions. This is dynamic equilibrium.

In some cases, plants absorb mineral ions against the force of diffusion. Energy is used in this process, which is called **active transport**. Large molecules cannot pass through selectively permeable membranes. Instead, they flow into pouches in the membrane and are sealed off. They then enter the cell in vacuoles.

Transpiration

Water sometimes has to rise great distances through the stem. The most important forces that cause this are transpiration and cohesion of water molecules in the very narrow xylem vessels. Transpiration is water loss by evaporation from leaves and stems, mainly through pores called **stomata**. As the plant loses water through its stomata, it takes in water through the roots by osmosis. The entire column of water in the xylem is pulled up the stem by evaporation. On warm days, the transpiration rate is high because it depends on the same factors as evaporation. Stomata open during the day and close during the night or when there is a shortage of water.

During the day, photosynthesis take place in the **guard cells** of the stomata.

This produces glucose which dissolves in the cells' vacuoles. There is now relatively more water in the surrounding cells than in the guard

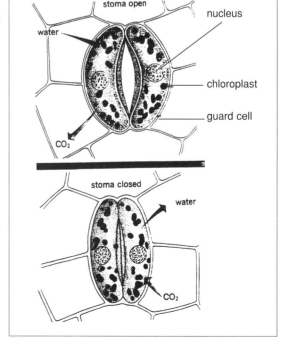

Stomata of a flowering plant

cells so the guard cells take in water by osmosis and swell, thus opening the pore. At night, no photosynthesis takes place, so there is no net flow of water into the guard cells and the pore closes.

Plant hormones

Hormones are of major importance in regulating the way that a plant grows. There are many groups of plant hormones, such as **auxins** and **gibberellins**.

Plants respond to their surroundings by growing either toward a stimulus (positive tropism) or away from one (negative tropism). This is done according to the hormonal effect on the growth of certain cells. Hormonal action is also affected by light and temperature changes. Commercial plant growers can control flowering and fruit ripening by means of artificial periods of light and darkness, as well as by application of certain hormones.

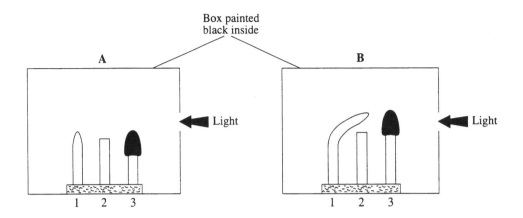

1   Diagram **A** shows an investigation to show the effect of light on the growth of oat shoots (coleoptiles). **B** shows the results one day later. Shoot 2 had the tip cut off; the tip of shoot 3 was covered with a cap of aluminium foil.

(a) Name the type of response shown in B.

.... (1)

(b) (i)   Which part of the oat shoot is sensitive to light ?

.... (1)

(ii) Give **two** reasons for your answer.

.... (2)

(c) (i)   What substance is responsible for the changes shown in B ?

.... (1)

(ii) Describe the effect of this substance on the shoots.

.... (1)

(iii) What is the effect of light on this substance ?

.... (1)

(d) State the purpose of the treatments given to shoots 2 and 3.

.... (1)

WJEC 1996

2 The graph shows the water loss from a plant during a hot windy day.

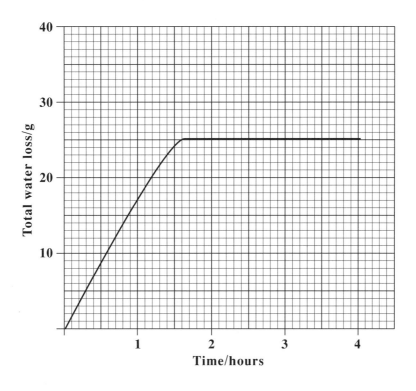

(a) Explain how the plant loses water.

....

....

....

.... (2)

(b) Explain why the plant might wilt two hours after the start of the experiment on a hot windy day.

....

....

....

.... (2)

(c) Draw a curve on the graph showing the water loss of the same plant during a hot humid day. (2)

NICCEA 1995

3 The table shows the results of an investigation in which small pieces of potato were placed in different concentrations of sugar solution.

% Concentration sugar solution	% Change in mass of potato
5	+8
10	+3
15	+1
20	-8
25	-11

Note that + means a mass increase and - means a mass decrease.

(a) Estimate the % concentration of sugar solution that would produce a 5% loss in mass.

.... (1)

(b) What concentration of sugar is closest to the concentration of the potato cell sap ?

.... (1)

(c) Name the biological process which would cause the loss or gain in mass.

.... (1)

(d) State two examples of the process in living organisms.

(i) ....

(ii) .... (2)

(e) Explain why some pieces of potato lost mass whereas others gained mass.

....

....

....

....

....

.... (4)

4   Four different potted plants. **A**, **B**, **C** and **D**, of the same species were used in an investigation.

Plant A was a variegated variety i.e. leaves with both green and non-green areas. The other plants were all of a non-variegated green variety. Plant B had been grown entirely in the dark. All four plants were placed in a dark cupboard for 48 hours. A starch test on a leaf taken from each of the plants A, B, C and D showed negative results.

Four test tubes labelled A, B, C and D were partly filled with the same amount of orange coloured hydrogencarbonate indicator solution (HCIS). A second leaf from each of the four plants was then placed in the appropriate test tube. The four leaves were approximately the same size. The test tubes were set up as shown below and were placed at equal distances from a bright light source for six hours.

HCIS containing an atmospheric concentration of carbon dioxide is orange-red in colour. At high carbon dioxide concentration it goes yellow. Lowering the dissolved carbon dioxide concentration results in a colour change from yellow to a purple-red/claret.

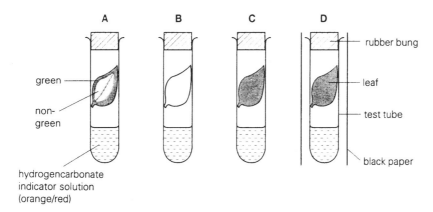

(a) The table shows the colour of the HCIS in each test tube at the end of the six hour period.

A	B	C	D
red	yellow	purple-red/claret	yellow

(i) Name the carbon dioxide absorbing process which occurs in leaf **C** but not in **D** and explain why the process does not happen in **D**.

....

....

.... (2)

(ii) Name another process which occurs in the leaves in both test tubes C and D and which causes the colour change in D. Why does the colour change occur?

....

....

.... (4)

(iii) Explain the difference in colour of the HCIS in test tubes A and C.

....

....

....

....

.... (4)

(b) After the six hours exposure to light, the leaves were taken from the test tube and tested for starch using iodine solution.

(i) The diagrams show the leaves after the starch test. Shade the leaves where appropriate to show the expected results.

    A   B   C   D

(2)

(ii) Explain the results you have shown for leaf **B**.

....

....

....

.... (3)

(c) What is the importance of the negative results obtained when testing the leaves for starch immediately after the plants had been in the dark for 48 hours?

....

....

....

.... (2)

MEG 1996

5 The diagram shows the lower part of a section through the leaf of a flowering plant.

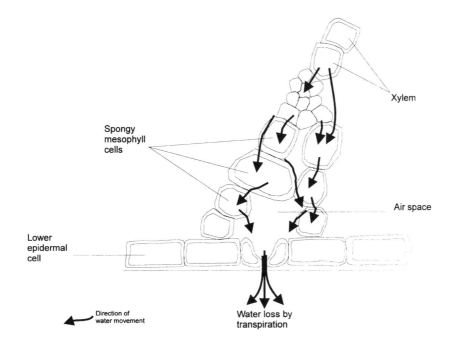

(a) (i) Not all of the water entering the leaf through the xylem is transpired through the stomata of the leaf. What happens to the water not transpired through the stomata?

....

....

.... (2)

QUESTIONS

(ii) Describe briefly how you could show that the water present in the xylem is the same water that was absorbed by the roots of the plant.

....

....

....

....

.... (3)

(iii) Name the support material, other than cellulose, present in the walls of the xylem vessels.

.... (1)

(iv) The cell walls of the spongy mesophyll cells are little more than thin layers of cellulose. Describe how these cells support the leaf.

....

....

....

.... (2)

(v) Describe how the loss of water vapour through the stomata contributes to the transport of materials from the roots to the leaves.

....

....

....

.... (2)

(b) The graph shows the relative size of the stomatal openings over a 24-hour period for a flowering plant growing in a temperate climate in early Summer.

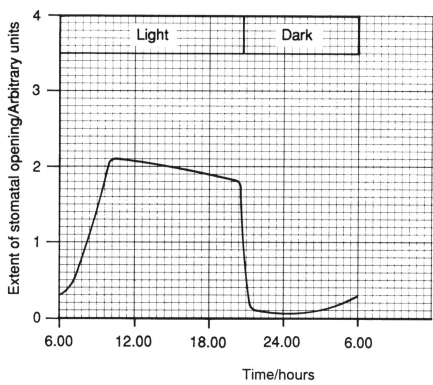

(i) Using the data in the graph above, describe what happens to the stomatal openings during the 24-hour period.

....

....

....

....

....

....

....

....

.... (5)

QUESTIONS

(ii) In temperate regions, temporary closure of the stomata may happen occasionally during daylight hours. Suggest an explanation for this fact.

....

....

....

.... (2)

(iii) In the tropics, closure of stomata for a period around midday is very common. State one disadvantage and one advantage to the plant of this behaviour.

Disadvantage ....

....

Advantage ....

.... (2)

(iv) Describe how osmosis may be involved in controlling the opening and closing of stomata.

....

....

....

....

....

....

....

....

....

....

.... (5)

1 LIFE PROCESSES

Question	Answer	Mark

1 (a) (i)

Part of digestive system	Letter
Liver	**H**
Pancreas	**C**
Oesophagus	**A**
Appendix	**G**

4

(ii) E is the colon and has the function of absorbing water from the indigestible material that it contains.

1

(iii) 1. Large surface area provided by villi. 2. Good blood supply.
(or A thin lining. Lacteals for digested fat absorption.)

2

(One mark each)

(b) (i)

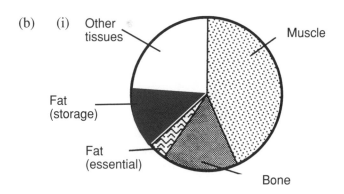

2

(ii) Muscle.   (iii) Female.   (iv) $\frac{45}{100}$ x 80 = 36kg.   1 mark for each

3

> **Examiner's tip**   Note that this is a typical question which involves knowledge of both structure and function. Do not attempt to learn how to draw a diagram of the digestive system. It is much more important to be able to label the parts and know the functions of the parts. In part (iii) there are more than two answers but do not waste your time writing more than two. Only the first two that you write will be marked. Part (b) is typical of a question that involves handling data and translating one form (a table) into another (a pie chart).

---

2 (a) (i) Amylase. (ii) Salivary glands or pancreas.   1 mark for each

2

(b) (i) An enzyme will have its own optimum pH for its action to proceed at the fastest rate. A pH above or below this optimum, will reduce the rate of the enzyme's action.

1

(ii)

	Statement numbers
The enzyme pepsin acts only on protein molecules.	3
Protein molecules are broken down to form short chains of amino acids.	5

2

> **Examiner's tip**   The question tests recall and understanding of the principles of enzyme action. Note that you must be very sure of your answer to (b)(ii). If you put all of the numbers in the boxes, the examiner will only mark the first. Look at the mark allocation for this part of the question. It is only 2. This implies that there are only two letters needed.

Question	Answer	Mark
3 (a)		2

Name	Function
Ligament	Holds the bones of a joint together
Cartilage	Reduces friction between bones at a joint
Synovial fluid	Lubricates the joint to reduce friction.

Question	Answer	Mark
(b)	Two muscles are needed to control movements of the bones of a hinge joint because they work in antagonistic pairs.	1
	While one is contracting, its partner is relaxing.	1

Examiner's tip   A common confusion is between a ligament and a tendon. Remember that a tendon connects a muscle to a bone. It will not be sufficient just to mention that muscles act in antagonistic pairs. For both marks, you will need to explain the meaning of the term.

Question	Answer	Mark
4 (a) (i)	The palisade layer.	1
(ii)	The upper epidermis.	1
(b)	The air spaces allow air with carbon dioxide to circulate throughout the leaf.	1
	They enable a large surface area to be present for gaseous exchange.	1
	They keep the air saturated to keep a moist surface area for gaseous exchange.	1

Examiner's tip   Part (a) relies on simple observation but part (b) requires knowledge of the features of an efficient surface for gaseous exchange. These are principles which apply to all such surfaces whether they are for breathing or photosynthesis.

Question	Answer	Mark
5 (a)	The pancreas.	1
(b)	Diabetes.	1
(c)	The pancreas must be able to produce insulin when it is needed.	
	The effects of injections of insulin soon wear off.	1
(d) (i)	The antibodies would react with insulin (because it is a protein like an antigen).	1
(ii)	The white blood cells would ingest (engulf) the insulin-secreting cells.	1
(e)	Insulin helps to regulate glucose.	1
	Insulin removes glucose from the blood.	1
	Glucagon helps to change glycogen into glucose.	1
(f)	Correct order is C, D, B, E, A.	5 x 1
(g)	It can be made in large quantities. It does not involve the killing of animals.	**Any one for 1 mark.**

Question	Answer	Mark

The question brings together three areas of your syllabus i.e. knowledge of blood sugar regulation, antibody – antigen reactions, and genetic engineering.

At this higher level, note that a complete coverage of the syllabus is essential. The temptation to concentrate on a limited number of topics must be resisted. Note that for part (e) it is easy to confuse glucagon with glycogen.

Also, note that part (f) carries 5 marks for a correct sequence of events. A thorough knowledge of the principles of genetic engineering is needed or almost all of the five marks will be lost.

6	(a)	(i)	Cortex	1
		(ii)	It has been reabsorbed into the blood.	1
		(iii)	Urine	1
	(b)	(i)	$270dm^3$	1
		(ii)	$40dm^3$	1
		(iii)	Reabsorption of water into the blood seems to be reduced.	1
		(iv)	Protein	1
	(c)		Diffusion	1
	(d)		It is the opposite to the direction of flow of the blood.	
			This helps to carry away the waste from the blood.	1
	(e)		They are too big to pass through the membrane.	1

Examiner's tip In order to answer part (a) it is necessary to relate the overall structure of the kidney to the microscopial detail of a single kidney tubule. You should familiarise yourself with a sectional view of a kidney as seen through a hand lens as well as the details of a single nephron (kidney tubule). The reabsorptive function of the kidney should be understood for parts (a) (ii) and (iii).

Part (b) requires graphical interpretation and is a popular method of assessing understanding kidney function.

The basic principles of a kidney machine are all that are required for parts (c) to (e).

---

2 INHERITANCE AND EVOLUTION

Question	Answer	Mark
1 (a)	Hormones are chemical secretions of ductless glands	1
	producing a definate physiological effect in the body.	1
(b) (i)	It is 'cut' out using enzymes.	1
(ii)	[A] A clone is genetically identical to its parent	1
	derived from a single individual by asexual reproduction.	1
	[B] They reproduce asexually	1
	very rapidly.	1

Question	Answer	Mark
	Bacteria can be cultured using cheap waste materials from industrial food manufacture.	1
(c)	It does not involve killing animals.	1
	There are many people whose cultural beliefs do not allow or agree with killing animals for human benefit.	1
	OR Because of mass production	1
	supply will keep up with demand.	1

> **Examiner's tip** (a) Note the importance of a concise definition here. Most candidates would have a knowledge of certain hormones and their effects, but it is not so easy to write a definition which applies to all animal produced hormones. NOT ALL hormones are concerned with growth and development.
> (b)(ii)[A] Again, a definition is needed. Two marks are available – 'genetically identical' and 'asexual reproduction' are the important points.
> [B] Do not fall into the trap of writing about the ethics of using animal-derived insulin here. There is scope for this in part (c).

Question	Answer	Mark
2 (a)	Homozygous – An individual receiving identical alleles from both its parents.	1
	Heterozygous – An individual receiving dissimilar alleles from both its parents.	1
(b) (i)	1 : 1.	1
(ii)	**Aa**	1

> **Examiner's tip** (a) Be prepared to define all of the genetical terms required by the syllabus that you are following. It is advisable to have a copy of the syllabus as a check list for your revision. (b) This short question tests an important concept of dominant and recessive characters. If **A** is dominant to a, then a cross between **AA** and **aa** would give all **Aa** offspring. The diagrams tell you that this is clearly not the case, so the parents must be **Aa** (normal) and **aa** (vestigial).

Question	Answer	Mark
3 (a)	C	1
(b)	Male	1
	blue eyes	1
(c) (i)	**bb**	1
(ii)	The gene for blue eyes is recessive. If Sarah had the B genes, she would have brown eyes.	1
(d) (i)	Lucy	1
(ii)	In order to be an identical twin to Rachel, the twin must be female and have the same genotype.	1
		1

Examiner's tip	This type of genetics question tests very basic principles and usually appears towards the beginning of the exam paper. It depends on knowledge of the term 'genotype' and also on an understanding of the meaning of IDENTICAL twins. The rest is straightforward interpretation of given data.

Question	**Answer**	**Mark**

4 (a) **(i)** The transfer of pollen from the anther to the stigma **1**
of a different flower of the same species. **1**

(ii) Because the parents were pure-bred (both homozygous) **1**
Red is dominant to white. **1**

(iii) Key: **R** = red (dominant). **r** = white (recessive) **1**
(for key)

Parents　　　　Genotypes　　**Rr**　x　**Rr**　　**1**
(for genotypes)

Phenotypes　　Red　　　Red　　**1**
(for phenotypes)

Gametes　　**R + r**　　**R + r**　　**1**
(for gametes)

F2

	R	r
R	RR red	Rr red
r	rR red	rr white

1
(for working)

F2 ratio　3 red to　1 white　　**1**

(b) **(i)** A mutation is a change in genetic makeup resulting in a new
characteristic that can be inherited. **1**
Here, a mutation of DNA could have taken place by the wrong pattern
of base pairs being produced when DNA duplicated itself (replication). **1**
DNA regulates the production of colour in the flower. **1**

(ii) The blue colour was an advantage to the species. **1**
More pollinating insects could have been attracted to the blue
colour than the red for pollination. **1**
Reproduction would ensure that the gene was passed on to
future generations. **1**

Examiner's tip	Plant reproduction and the principles of Mendel's Law of Segregation (Mendel's 1st Law) are brought together in this question which involves problem solving and an understanding of the principle of Natural Selection.

The layout of the answer to the genetics problem can vary – it need not be in the box form as indicated, but the Examiner will want you to show that you understand the principles clearly. Note the distribution of the six marks for a step-by-step logical approach.
You will not have studied evolution in relation to the particular species mentioned here. Again, it is the application of principles, (probably learned through the work of Darwin) that is important. You can see how the Examiner is testing understanding rather than recall.

3 POPULATIONS AND HUMAN INFLUENCES

Question	Answer	Mark
1 (a) (i)	0–4	1
(ii)	4%	1
(iii)	Poor health care/hygiene.	1
	Poor diet/malnutrition.	1
	Poor quality housing/living standards.	1
(b) (i)	There are more females living over 55 years of age.	1
(ii)	The birth rate is higher in 1840/the adult death rate is higher in 1840 *or* the birth rate is lower in 1970/the adult death rate is lower in 1970.	1
(iii)	Shortage of food/spread of disease/lack of housing/pollution/ unemployment/destruction of habitats.	2 × 1

> **Examiner's tip** Note that three of the marks can be obtained without any biological knowledge – just by interpreting the data. However, a knowledge of how to interpret population statistics is part of the National Curriculum.

Question	Answer	Mark
2 (a) (i)	Photosynthesis.	1
(ii)	Respiration or decay.	1
(iii)	Coal.	1

> **Examiner's tip** It was difficult to understand this question. The examiner would never write a 'trick question'. Do not be put off if the answer seems obvious.

Question	Answer	Mark
(iv)	Road transport.	1
(b) (i)	The Greenhouse Effect.	1
(ii)	Large amounts of carbon dioxide (and other greenhouse gases) are trapped under the ozone layer.	1
	The sun's rays (short-wave solar radiation) enter the Earth's atmosphere. Some of this is absorbed by the Earth.	1
	Long-wave radiation is reflected back towards space but is reflected back down to Earth by the greenhouse gases.	1
	This causes a heating up of the Earth's surface.	1

> **Examiner's tip** The Greenhouse Effect and the depletion of the ozone layer are often confused by candidates. Make sure you know the difference between the two processes.

Question	Answer	Mark

3 (a) (i) 1 mark for each correctly drawn bar on the graph. | **3**

(ii) methane | **1**
carbon dioxide. | **1**

Examiner's tip The question did not ask for two gases; however, the question did refer to 'gases' and the (2) indicates two marks available. If you were unsure and wrote more than two gases for your answer you would lose marks. For every extra incorrect answer given, one mark is cancelled from your total for that part of the question.

(iii) If there were more renewable energy devices such as windmills in operation then less fossil fuel would need to be burned in the electricity generating process. If homes were better insulated then less fuel would be needed to heat the houses.

Both of these examples would reduce the amount of carbon dioxide entering the atmosphere. Carbon dioxide has the largest influence on the Greenhouse Effect.

If homes were better insulated there would also be less use of air conditioning systems. These systems contain CFCs, which also have an influence on the Greenhouse Effect.

Green plants take in carbon dioxide as they photosynthesize; therefore, if more trees were planted, more carbon dioxide would be removed from the atmosphere. Carbon dioxide has a major influence on the Greenhouse Effect. | **6**

Examiner's tip When you study this question you will notice that there are three statements to discuss and six marks available. The answer to each statement, if extended, is worth two marks. If the answer is correct, but vague or too brief, then only one mark would be awarded.

This type of answer would only be credited with three marks:

Renewable energy should be used so less electricity is made. Houses need to be better insulated so less fuel is used for central heating. If more trees were planted more carbon dioxide would be removed from the atmosphere.

(b) (i) 350
     280 −
     ‾‾‾‾
     70 parts per million. | **1**

(ii) In the year 2030 the population will be much greater, therefore:
there will be a greater demand for electricity and more fossil fuels will be burned.

or

more buildings will be needed so there will be an increase in the amount of cement being produced and more forests will be destroyed to create space for housing and crops. | **1**

These factors will increase the amount of carbon dioxide in the atmosphere. | **1**

---

4 (a) (i) In experiment A the bag was filled with air.
In experiment B the bag was filled with sulphur dioxide. | **1**

(ii) The control was set up to show that any effect on the cress seedlings

Question	Answer	Mark
	was due to the presence of sulphur dioxide,	1
	otherwise a similar effect would be shown in the control.	1
(iii)	Individual seedlings may grow higher (forced) than others or die.	1
	Averaged results are more reliable in showing a pattern.	1
(b)	All 5 bars correct	3
	4 bars correct	2
	3–2 bars correct	1

> **Examiner's tip** Room has been left on the grid for you to draw in your bar chart. Always enter your answer onto the grid provided.

Question	Answer	Mark
(c) (i)	Group 3	1
	The results for Experiments A and B are the same.	1
	This suggests that there is air in both bags or a hole in Bag B.	1
(ii)	Sulphur dioxide affects plant growth,	1
	causing plants to be shorter in length.	1
	This is supported by the results of the control.	1
	The average height of the seedlings in Bag A is greater than the average height in Bag B.	1
(iii)	The sulphur dioxide reacts with the water in the atmosphere to form sulphuric acid.	1
	This falls as acid rain,	1
	which affects plant life and animal life in lakes.	1
	Acid rain also corrodes buildings.	1

> **Examiner's tip** You would need to plan out this answer in rough first and check that you have four main points. Then write out your answer neatly.

Question	Answer	Mark
5 (a)	The drought would evaporate the water and concentrate the lead.	1
(b)	The lead affected the nervous system	1
	which supplied the muscles of the trunk.	1
(c)	The lead would be concentrated through food chains	1
	and enter humans in the diet via fish.	1
(d)	Correct order from top to bottom is D, E, B, G.	4 × 1

> **Examiner's tip** This is an example of a question which asks you to apply your knowledge of the effects of heavy metal poisoning to an unfamiliar situation. In order to prepare yourself for this type of question, it is essential to understand rather than learn by re-call. The context of the topic could be almost any situation where humans pollute the environment with heavy metals. However, note that a lot of information is given in the beginning of the question. This requires comprehension. For part (d), you are required to interpret data in the form of a graph. This is a very popular technique in setting questions on population changes.

4 ECOSYSTEMS

Question	Answer	Mark
1 (a)	Algae → Snails → Caddis larvae → Diving beetles OR Pondweed → hog lice → Caddis larvae→ Diving beetles	
	The marks are for: the correct sequence and direction of arrows.	1 1
(b) (i)	Light. Temperature. Number of herbivores. Mineral concentration. Number of carnivores (indirectly).　　1 for each of any 4	4
(ii)	Water fleas would increase because there would be more food for them The mussels would increase because there would be more algae and waterfleas for them to eat.	1 1 1 1
(c)	2 loach 30 snails Algae	1 1
(d)	Oxygen is used by the animals and plants in respiration but is produced by plants in photosynthesis. Carbon dioxide is used by plants in photosynthesis but is produced by animals and plants during respiration.	1 1

> **Examiner's tip** Part (a) is a very popular way of testing the understanding of food webs and food chains. It is essential to indicate the correct direction of the arrows because this is the only way that you can show the direction of energy flow. Part (b) requires an understanding of the feeding relationships within this community. It shows how the population of one species is dependent on another. (c) Note that you need to know how to translate the numerical data into a pyramid of number. Sometimes data is given so that you can make a pyramid of biomass. (Mass of living material per unit area or volume.) Finally, in part (d), there is opportunity to show how animals depend on plants and vice versa. – the basic principle of ecology.

Question	Answer	Mark
2 (a)	The Sun.	1
(b)	Temperature, pH, Water, oxygen	any 3 × 1
(c) (i)	30 000	1
(ii)	When the birth rate and death rate are equal or the maximum number of a species that can be supported in a given habitat without affecting the population of other species.	1
(iii)	1915.	1
(iv)	It rose gradually and then very sharply. The probable reason was that the predators were killed and the conditions for feeding and reproducing were favourable.	1 1

> **Examiner's tip** Predator-prey relationships provide plenty of data that examiners can use to set questions on this topic. Note that most of the answers require interpretation of graphical data in this case. The context may be unfamiliar, but the principles will be the same for any habitat.

Question	Answer	Mark
3 (a)	A lacewing fly. B hawk or fox. C fox. D caterpillars.	4×1
(b)	<u>PRODUCER</u>	
(c) (i)	Sunlight	1
(ii)	Photosynthesis.	1
(d)	The weasels would decrease in number.	1
	The plants would increase in number.	1
(e)	The voles would decrease	1
	because there would be more predators	1
	which would compete with the weasels.	1

Examiner's tip Part (a) requires careful interpretation of given data. At first, you might think that C could be a fox or a weasel but a careful consideration shows you that the weasel is already given in the food web. However, part B has two alternatives according to the data in the table. Caterpillars for D have to be deduced from the data and not directly read from the table. The table shows that only voles eat plants. Parts (b) and (c) require knowledge but (d) and (e) test your skills at interpreting the given data.

Question	Answer	Mark
4 (a)	X Excretion	1
	Y Respiration	1
(b)	$\dfrac{150}{2500} \times 100$ (1 mark for method) $= 6\%$ (1 mark for answer)	2
(c)	There is energy lost at each feeding level.	1
	By the end of a food chain with five links, there is not enough energy left to support another feeding level.	1

Examiner's tip In order to answer part (a), be careful to note the terms 'wastes' and 'heat' at the beginning of the question. Don't forget your calculator for part (b). You will gain a mark for showing that you know the correct method, even if the answer is wrong.

5 MICROBES AND MANKIND

Question	Answer	Mark
1 (a) (i)	Decay is the breakdown of organic material	1
	by microbes.	1
(ii)	Bacteria or Fungi	1
(b)	Nitrification is the build up of nitrites and nitrates from ammonium compounds,	1

Question			Answer	Mark
			by nitrifying bacteria.	1
	(c)		Nitrogen	1
	(d)	(i)	Peas and beans have nitogen fixing bacteria in their roots.	1
			These can make nitrates using nitrogen from the atmosphere.	1
		(ii)	They use the animals' excretory products as a source of nitrogen for the nitrogen cycle.	1

Examiner's tip Candidates often find the concept of the nitrogen cycle difficult. This may be because they try to learn the flow chart of the cycle without really understanding it. Questions will concentrate on the role of the bacteria involved in the cycle and this is no exception. It is useful to realise that there are four types of bacteria involved. These are: putrefying, nitrifying, nitrogen-fixing, and denitrifying. You should learn and understand the function of each type. The names of the species of bacteria are not required to be known.

Question			Answer	Mark
2	(a)	(i)	As a control, to show that the sugar was responsible for carbon dioxide production.	1
		(ii)	Sugar S.	1
		(iii)	To remove all the air and to have the same conditions at the start.	1
		(iv)	Because the sugar was used up.	1
	(b)		Raise the temperature to the optimum for yeast.	1
			Replace as it is being used.	1
	(c)		Q and R.	1
			Yeasts do not naturally occur in animals and do not use them for fermentation.	1

Examiner's tip This may be an unfamiliar experiment to you but it is really about principles of fermentation by yeast. Note that the concepts of a control and experimental procedure must be understood. The use of yeast in biotechnology is a popular topic for questions.

Question			Answer	Mark
3	(a)	(i)	To remove any floating material.	1
		(ii)	**B** Settlement of sludge to the bottom of the liquid.	1
			C Killing harmful microbes by increasing oxygen via aeration.	1
			D Anaerobic digestion of sludge by microbes.	1
	(b)	(i)	Methane	1
		(ii)	It is used as fertiliser on land.	1
	(c)		Nitrifying bacteria	1
	(d)		Sewage contains nitrates. These are used by plants for growth.	
			The plants grow so quickly that they would pile up on top of one another.	

Question	Answer	Mark
	Those at the bottom die because of lack of light.	
	Bacteria would cause these to decay and so take oxygen from the water.	2

6 PLANT BIOLOGY

Question			Answer	Mark
1	(a)		Phototropism.	1
	(b)	(i)	The tip.	1
		(ii)	The shoot does not respond when the tip is removed.	1
			The tip does not respond when it is covered.	1
	(c)	(i)	A hormone (Auxin).	1
		(ii)	It causes the cells to elongate.	1
		(iii)	It causes the hormone to move away from light (to the part exposed to least light).	1
	(d)		As a control, to show that it is the tip that responds to light.	1

		Answer	Mark
2	(a)	Plants lose water because of evaporation	1
		through stomata and the cuticle of both stems and leaves.	1
	(b)	Wilting occurs when the rate of water loss by evaporation exceeds	1
		the rate of water entry through the roots due to osmosis.	1
	(c)	The curve should follow the shape of the one given but it should be below the line shown	1
		and should level off in the same way.	1
3	(a)	Any number between 16 and 19.	1
	(b)	15%	1

Question	Answer	Mark
(c)	Osmosis.	1
(d)	The movement of water into roots.	1
	The movement of water into guard cells when stomata open.	1
	(OR the diffusion of water through the lining of the intestine in animals or the re-absorption of water in the kidney tubules)	
(e)	The potato tissue would lose mass when water passed out from the cells,	1
	from where it was in relatively high concentration,	1
	to where it was in relatively low concentration;	1
	through the selectively permeable cell membrane.	1
	The same marks would be given for the opposite explanation when the potato gained mass.	

Examiner's tip Parts (a) and (b) require deduction from the data. The rest requires knowledge and understanding of the principles of diffusion and osmosis. Common errors in part (e) are descriptions of solutions (rather than water) passing through a selectively permeable membrane, and a statement that the cell wall (rather than the cell membrane) is selectivley permeable.

Question	Answer	Mark
4 (a) (i)	Photosynthesis	1
	This process did not occur in D because light energy is required for photosynthesis to take place.	1

Examiner's tip In most experiments investigating photosynthesis, the usual variable to control is light.

(ii)	Respiration occurs in both C and D.	1
	Respiration produces carbon dioxide.	1
	As no photosynthesis is taking place no carbon dioxide is removed.	1
	In high carbon dioxide concentration HCIS turns yellow.	1

Examiner's tip You must ensure that you have your facts correct before you start to write down this answer. Read the information again, then plan your answer out in rough, and check that you have the 4 facts. Then write your answer out neatly.

(iii)	Leaf C has more chlorophyll than leaf A	1
	so more photosynthesis took place in leaf C.	1
	More photosynthesis requires more carbon dioxide to be absorbed,	1
	less carbon dioxide in C causes HCIS indicator to turn purple-red.	1

Examiner's tip Again check your 4 facts before you start to write your answer.

Question	Answer	Mark

(b) (i)

A   B   C   D

blue/black —

brown —

All four correctly shaded in.   **2**
(Only two or three shaded in correctly = 1 mark)
(Only one shaded correctly = 0 marks)

> **Examiner's tip**   The shaded area must be clearly marked, particularly on leaf A.

(ii) Plant B was kept in the dark so no chlorophyll developed,   **1**
this means photosynthesis was prevented,   **1**
therefore no starch was produced.   **1**

> **Examiner's tip**   Many canlidates did not read the question carefully and explained the results for all the leaves, instead of just leaf B. These candidates failed to gain credit for their answers. Always read the question carefully.

(c)   This shows that the leaf did not contain any starch before
the experiment,   **1**
therefore any starch formed must have been produced by
photosynthesis during the experiment.   **1**
This made it a fair test or a control.   **1**

(Any two)

> **Examiner's tip**   Questions concerning experiments usually ask about the control. Make sure you understand the reasons for a control in an experiment.

5 (a) (i) It is used for photosynthesis   **1**
and to maintain pressure in cell vacuoles for support.   **1**

(ii) Place a complete flowering plant (with roots attached) into a solution of
harmless coloured dye.   **1**
Leave it for a day.   **1**
Examine a section through the stem and note the presence of
the coloured dye in the xylem.   **1**

(iii) Lignin.   **1**

(iv) Their vacuoles are filled with cell sap.   **1**
This provides pressure which supports the cells.   **1**

(v) The evaporation of water vapour through the stomata acts as a suction
which draws up water through the xylem.   **1**
This suction is transmitted through the stem to the roots.   **1**

Question		Answer	Mark
(b)	(i)	Between 6 a.m. and 11a.m. the stomata open.	1
		They then start to close when the light is at its maximum.	1
		They close gradually until about 21.00hrs	1
		and then very rapidly until 22.00 hrs.	1
		Most remain closed until about 4 a.m., when they begin to open again.	1
	(ii)	During daylight it is possible for the rate of water loss to be more than the rate of water entry.	1
		Stomata then close to protect against wilting.	1
	(iii)	Disadvantage: Transpiration will stop and the cooling effect will not take place.	1
		OR	
		Minerals will not be transported to the leaves for photosynthesis.	
		Advantage: Wilting will be prevented.	1
	(iv)	The guard cells contain chloroplasts which are used in photosynthesis during daylight to produce glucose.	1
		This is dissolved in the cell sap making a concentrated solution of sugar.	1
		The surrounding cells have a more dilute solution as cell sap, so water passes into the guard cells by osmosis.	1
		The cells swell away from the pore of the stomata and so the pore opens.	1
		During darkness, no photosynthesis takes place so no glucose can be made to form a concentrated solution and the pores close.	1

Examiner's tip This is an example of how one question can test a topic in a great deal of depth. It is unusual to have such a long question carrying so many marks, but such questions can occur on higher tier papers. It serves to illustrate the fact that in order to opt to attempt the higher tier, you really have to know and understand topics in detail. You are advised to obtain a copy of the syllabus that you are following to check the detail necessary for the examination. There is emphasis on both the transporting and support role of water in a plant in part (a). In part (b)(i) note that you are asked to describe what happens to the stomatal openings as seen from the graph. You are not asked to explain 'how' they open. In part (iv) you have a chance to demonstrate your knowledge of osmosis and apply it to stomatal action.